EXPLORING
MEDIA
& CULTURAL STUDIES

Kendall Hunt
publishing company

METASEBIA
WOLDEMARIAM

www.kendallhunt.com
Send all inquiries to:
4050 Westmark Drive
Dubuque, IA 52004-1840

Copyright © 2015 by Kendall Hunt Publishing Company

ISBN 978-1-4652-4835-0

Printed in the United States of America

CONTENTS

SECTION 1 – UNDERSTANDING MEDIA

SECTION 2 – EVOLVING MEDIA ISSUES

SECTION 3 – EXPLORING CULTURAL STUDIES

SECTION 1
Understanding Media

CHAPTER 1

The Evolution of Media

> "The future of media is already here."
>
> —Henry Blodget

A Brief History of Visual Communication

Numerous books, research articles, and cultural commentaries trace the development of communication and examine how human invention and technology have modified how we tell our stories (Rogers, 1994). Here, we will describe that detailed and lengthy evolution in five primary stages: pictures, the written word or text, still images, moving images and, finally, the digital revolution and its ever-growing platforms that merge all media.

Pictorial Communication: Telling Stories With Hand-Created Pictures and Signs

We visualized the world around us and translated it pictographically long before we wrote. Paleolithic man used vision to survive: Hunters followed the tracks of antelope, bison, and other animals for food. The hoof marks were graphic signs of real animals whose images in turn were etched and painted on cave walls. Essentially, those petroglyphs and pictographs recorded the hunt. The images offer a graphic depiction of the hunt and other compelling stories of our ancestors creating a basic existence. The earliest forms of visual communication involved the drawing of intricate pictures, which served as the earliest alphabets. Although we don't tend to think of letters or symbols as "visuals" today, if we think of the earliest graphic depictions of thoughts and events, we can understand that early alphabets were highly pictorial and visual.

Anthropologists believe that imagery embellished other related stories. Theories about that narrative meaning, they believe, related to magical powers imbued through the pictures, ritual, or even history and more practical applications. Any way you interpret that visualization, the cave art reveals a great deal about the creativity and ingenuity of its creators. Color, used to make the imagery more realistic, was concocted by mixing charcoal and various oxides together as pigment. Animal fat was merged with the coloring and applied by hand with sticks, reeds, and other tools to create the pictures. Imagine the thought, perseverance, and experimentation that had to have preceded that artistic and pragmatic solution.

Paleolithic Art Meaning and Debate

· · · · · · · · · · · · · ·

http://www.columbia.edu/itc/anthropology/v1007/2002projects/artcreation_files/3.htm

Early Block Printing in Asia

· · · · · · · · · · · · · ·

http://afe.easia.columbia.edu/song/tech/printing.htm

Later, our use of signs became more sophisticated. Literal renderings of things took on deeper, more abstract, and refined meaning. Pictures evolved into symbols to extend the written possibilities of language, connotation, and context, all through *signs*. Together, graphic marks could be arranged to convey ideation and narrative. For example, Sumerians and Egyptians recorded the history and culture of early civilizations graphically. Their narratives used visual communication and, along with it, a meticulous display of flat design. Later, more formal hieroglyphics that only the priests and a select few could read morphed into the more commonly used **demotic** ("of the people") **script**. That adaptation largely occurred to accommodate the needs of commerce and over time contributed to the development of the written word and eventually the use of text for communicating.

Words are the means to share what writers envision, a lens through which we focus, see, and understand stories authors present to us. For example, think about how your mind's eye forms a picture of a business associate with whom you have only an online and phone relationship. How this individual communicates with you fuels your imagination. However, the words themselves lead to some internalization of who this person is and what he or she must look like; it's the visual impressions the words bring to you as well as the mental landscapes they help create within when interacting.

Over time, oral storytelling and pictorial design as a means of recording messages took on the form of hand-written text in manuscripts and books. Occasionally, inscribed illustration and decorative lettering graced pages—all visual nuances to enhance storytelling. However, the number of books and manuscripts that scribes created were extremely limited—as were those having access to them. For the most part, the few who could read had to travel to small exclusive libraries. Early on, audiences consisted largely of nobility, clerics, scribes, and the other educated few; consequently, the most important information and knowledge lay guarded and hidden away. It was controlled largely by those who possessed it and by those who could read.

Eventually, scribes integrated more pictorial imagery into their writing; though largely illustrative, it helped enliven the story. Woodblock, although an old technology, was the next visual wrinkle to figure into graphic communication and storytelling. Initially merged into written manuscripts, a **woodblock** or woodcut was a hand-carved, squared off piece of wood that was inked and applied to pages.

Block printing originated in China, and its basic technique was passed on through the Egyptians. In medieval times, block-books combined text and images and were cut into a single woodblock. The text that accompanied the imagery in block printing was carved as well; this medium first appeared in Europe in the early 15th century.

Content varied in block printing from simple stories to playing cards. Typically, short allegories or parables told a simple story on a single page. However, stories could be hand bound into books containing up to 50 pages. Although originally reserved for nobility, the simple technology soon brought content to the masses and a cheaper alternative to books produced by scribes. Remember, too, that most of the common people at this time were illiterate and understood stories solely from pictures. Block printing had great appeal and represented the most graphic approach to storytelling to date for the masses, and, again, it did so at a price many could afford. Block printed materials were very much in demand.

The Invention and Adoption of the Printing Press: Telling Stories With Movable Type

Between the years of 1453 and 1456, Johannes Gutenberg invented modern printing. The first book off his press was the Bible. Using a simple wine press and moveable metal type, Gutenberg forever changed the evolution of storytelling—and human communication. Printing quickly spread across Europe. England's first printer, William Caxton, put the first two folios of Chaucer's *Canterbury Tales* to page in 1478 and 1483. At the end of the 15th century, there were more than 1,000 printers in Europe. By then, nearly 20 million books had been printed from more than 35,000 titles. That publishing achievement did not include advertising, posters, tracts, and other materials. The printing press was the first development to enable mass communication.

The Gutenberg Revolution

• • • • • • • • • • • • •

http://www.history.com/topics/middle-ages/videos/the-book-that-changed-the-world

However, printing was still an expensive proposition and a fledgling technology. Like any new medium, its true potential for reaching huge audiences was initially quite limited. Elitists mocked printed work, calling it vulgar and a fad doomed to failure; they continued to accumulate hand-written manuscripts. However, with time, printing and printed materials became increasingly supported and adopted by the masses—at a cost to calligraphers and others who worked with hand-written books. Even in late medieval times, new technology would eliminate jobs in the old technology.

Indeed, Gutenberg's printing press ushered in an era of mass communication, and with it the democratization of media. Books made knowledge more available than ever before, and printed materials were portable and mass produced. What once was available to a privileged few now was reaching the masses. Books helped establish small communities of people with similar interests. The wider availability of books and other printed materials led to improved literacy in Europe. Printed books and other publications not only informed larger numbers of people, they had a profound effect on education, politics, religion, philosophy, the arts, and sciences. Literacy and the knowledge it kindled brought with it many new ideas. It also established communication as an important business; from it books, advertising, and journalism would emerge. Wendell Phillips characterized the impact of moveable type and the printing press: "What gunpowder did for war the printing press has done for the mind" (Phillips, 1884, p. 40).

Eventually, the use of the printing press led to one of the oldest and historically most influential delivery formats for textual communication: the newspaper. Newspapers serve as a compendium of our collective daily lives. They provide information on many subjects and from many perspectives and geographic locations including business, sports, politics, entertainment, weather, and the arts. The newspaper is a visual medium. It integrates photography, typography, color, and design with words for storytelling. Its text fleshes out the stories, so it is an appropriate medium for longer and more detailed treatment of the news. Contemporary newspapers have become significantly more graphic since their inception. For example, over time, they featured bigger photos, adopted bolder graphic designs, invented Sunday magazine inserts, and later developed special sections to attract niche markets and the advertising they would attract. New, high-speed presses reduced labor costs and delivered a better, cleaner, and more efficiently produced newspaper.

In 1982, Gannett launched *USA Today*, which revolutionized the concept of "newspaper." Its generous use of color, information-graphics, and photography would become a model for many newspapers. *USA Today* was also the first newspaper to scale back the length of its stories. It delivered simple, quick articles accompanied by simple, appealing visuals. They first used color strategically with different colors for different sections. The move appealed to those who didn't have the time for a deep read. *USA Today* and its short articles and colorful design made sense for a population of readers that was increasingly busy and mobile. Despite critics claiming the paper had dummied down the news with sound bite content, Gannett's experiment realized immediate payoffs.

Other newspapers began to copy *USA Today*'s formula of succinct content and bright design in the hopes of attracting more readers and thus more advertising dollars. The move didn't turn around the mounting financial woes of the industry. To save money, the industry tried to save money in a number of ways: layoffs, a smaller broadsheet format to reduce paper and ink costs, and ultimately, reduced page count. But nothing seemed to work. Newspaper sales and subscriptions continued to plummet. The industry has also been affected by news media, advertising, technology, and the Internet. For a long time the newspaper industry dominated news dissemination and maintained an unchallenged grip on advertising. However, changes such as digital media have endangered the future of traditional newspaper publishing and forced many out of print. For instance, the *Seattle Post-Intelligencer* (Richman & James, 2009) and the *Christian Science Monitor* (Cook, 2008) publish online-only versions and have ceased print publication. Today, virtually all newspapers have online counterparts.

The effect of the printing press was astounding. It facilitated access to knowledge, led to the creation of libraries and specialized arts, sciences, and even the technologies that would advance visual communication in myriad ways. From handwriting on vellum to the height of the newspaper's astonishing power and influence, words remain at the core of all communication.

Still Images: Telling Stories With Photography

Words remain the core of most business communication. Consider newsletters, memos, emails, user instructions, messages exchanged on the corporate Internet, and stories published in industry-specific periodicals. Although words remain the quickest way to flesh out and hold fast to our immediate thoughts and needs, they can't visually reproduce reality the way photography can.

Photography

Photography captures place, people, things—anything that can be seen and even a few things that can't be seen. In that sense, it captures space and anything within it. Another inherent property of photography is that it stops time. Photographs are exposed and made in fractions of seconds, so photography captures a moment to record that face, place, or space as a splinter of time suspended forever within its frame.

Two Frenchmen, Joseph Niépce and Louis Daguerre, perfected a silver, iodine, and mercury process to stabilize a camera's latent image (1838) and made the first stabilized positive photographic image via the daguerreotype (Barger & White, 2000). Like so many media achievements, Daguerre's breakthrough was discovered by accident, and his first successful image took nearly eight hours to properly expose—an eternity by today's standards.

About the same time (1841), Englishman William Talbot invented the calotype. One of the primary differences from Daguerre's procedures was that Talbot used a negative process that could produce multiple positive photographs from the same image. That was an incredible breakthrough, because it allowed a photographer the opportunity to reproduce any number of photos from a single exposure. Talbot's regenerative process officially made multiple prints possible. A new medium was taking its first steps. Further experiments by Talbot and others moved the photographic process through glass negatives, calotype, collodion, platinotype, and other stages.

With these two major developments, **photography** (or light writing) was born. Not long after its discovery, photography was soon adopted for a wide variety of purposes that varied from humble family scrapbooks to portraiture, documentary, advertising, journalism, and art. Photography was embraced formally by the Academy of Science and used as a tool for documentation in everything from anthropology to medicine. It also had a huge impact on the arts, especially the naturalist and impressionist painters. Indeed, many artists took up photography, Degas among them. All photography is narrative in nature and has an inherent storytelling power—no matter the form it takes. Its major genres include portraiture, documentary, photojournalism, fashion, advertising, landscape, and fine art. Each of these areas possesses inherent narrative qualities. One of the most influential forms of photography has been photojournalism.

World's First Photograph

http://www
.youtube.com/watch?
v=78KfCkCN3ck

Photojournalism

As its name implies, **photojournalism** is a news medium that integrates journalism with the visual medium of photography. Photojournalism, via pictorial magazines and other publications, became the major visual news source for Americans from 1930 to the late 1960s. Magazines such as *Life*, *Look*, *Survey Graphic* and other pictorial magazines of the 1930s ushered in the "Golden Age of Photojournalism" and bridged that era into the 1960s. CNN, "on the scene" live reporting, and blogging did not yet exist. Americans mourning the assassination of President Kennedy saw grainy black and white video on the news and in their daily newspapers of images such as his casket, his grieving widow, and his young son's iconic salute. However, when their issue of *Life* or *Look* arrived, the images came alive in color, embedded within powerfully written accounts. *Life* and publications like it changed how people looked at the world by employing some of the world's finest photojournalists and documentary photographers. *Life*'s founder, Henry Luce, made the publication's mission clear: "To see life; to see the world; to eyewitness great events" (quoted in Kobre, 2004, p. 356).

Photo essays like the ones published in *Life* were, during this era, the most powerful form of visual communication and storytelling. Photojournalism brought the world into American living rooms via still photographs and served as one of the primary visual media available at that time. Times have changed, but our fascination with photography and its storytelling capacity have not. Today most of us have at least one digital camera. Blogs and sites like Pinterest and Facebook are full of still images captured and immediately uploaded of peoples' meals, sights seen on trips, gardens, home improvement projects, birthday celebrations, and more. We'll look at the impact of the digital age on photography in an upcoming section.

Moving Images: Telling Stories With Film

Moving images, or **motion pictures**, are comprised of a series of discrete frames projected in normal speed at a rate of 24 frames per second, which creates the illusion of motion. Film is used to both entertain and inform. Although we tend to think of film in terms of cinema, moving images are used in the production of TV journalism as well.

Although the history of moving pictures dates back to 1895, the first worldwide exhibition and acceptance of the medium came in 1927 with the release of the commercial film *The Jazz Singer* (Cousins, 2006). The moving picture, or film, is a powerful and complex form of visual communication that not only sets the agenda for what viewers think and talk about but also allows viewers to create and shape meaning based on what they have seen. Films tell stories about social and political institutions; they portray issues of critical importance including marriage, family, working life, racism, sexism, abuse, and heroism. Films both set the tone for society and reflect society's "temperature" on a particular issue at any given time. For example, when the film *12 Angry Men* was first released in 1957, it portrayed just that: twelve white men deliberating the fate of a boy from an inner-city slum accused of stabbing his father to death. The 1997 remake of the classic film was characterized by a more racially diverse jury, and a different set of complex social issues were used to describe the defendant's circumstances. In these ways, the film reflected society but also contributed to society's "discussion" about race, power, and criminal justice.

The Digital Revolution: Telling Stories Through Computers and the Internet

The Internet has become our primary conduit to all our other media today: Many watch television shows at hulu.com; we post our resumes and reach out to former, current, and potential colleagues at LinkedIn; we express our creativity by posting videos on YouTube and blogging; we use WebEx to meet with business associates around the block or the globe; some of us shop online more often than we go to the mall; we download our books from the Internet; read our news at traditional newspapers' and television outlets' websites; and we maintain some of our most personal relationships on Facebook. In fact, the era in which we live and communicate has been dubbed "The Facebook Revolution," (Vogelstein, 2007), a moniker that describes the profound effect a wide range of social, online media have had on society. In an interview with Diane Sawyer, Facebook founder Mark Zuckerberg described Facebook's appeal: "Right now, with social networks and other tools on the Internet, all of these 500 million people have a way to say what they're thinking and have their voice be heard" (Heussner, 2010). Interestingly, Facebook and other social media are unique in their capacity to allow our voices to be "heard" through a range of visual cues. For example, Facebook's recent visual interface shifted to the individual user "timeline," which encourages users to "tell your life story through photos, friendships, and personal milestones like graduating or traveling to new places" (Facebook, 2012).

Whatever you prefer to call it—Digital Age, Computer Age, or Information Age—it has been hailed as a revolution, and it is primarily visual. Today's mass media use wireless communication technology across the world to connect an intricate network of various kinds of communications systems. **Digital media** refer to electronic channels that operate on digital, as opposed to analog codes. Digital media can carry photographs and other visual images, including text, audio, and video. A contemporary understanding of "new" digital media further implies that digital content is available on demand—any time, any place where an Internet connection is available, using our computers, tablets, or smartphones.

The Computer

Two major inventions and their evolved improvements made this revolution possible: the computer and the Internet. Over the years, scientists, media professionals, and inventors developed numerous breakthroughs in computer language, storage, mainframe computers, software, networking, robots, artificial intelligence, and microprocessors. That is a very short list of areas where substantial changes were realized. For a readable overview of the history of the computer up to the personal computer, see Aspray and Campbell-Kelly (1997).

Arguments exist over who invented the computer. Most scholars attribute that accomplishment to inventor, professor, and physicist Dr. John Atanasoff and his graduate assistant, Clifford Berry (Mollenhoff, 1988). Although its circuitry wouldn't run a hand calculator today, the first computer was colossal in size. Their computer, which was developed at Iowa State (1937–1942), was a hulk of a machine—too wide to get through the door of their lab. The 700-pound ABC machine used 300 vacuum tubes and roughly 5,000 feet of wire. By comparison, too, it could process only 1,500 bits per second. That said, the ABC computer shared three crucial characteristics with modern computers: It used a binary system; it performed calculations electronically; and its system kept the memory component separate from its computation counterpart.

George Dyson and the Birth of the Computer

http://www.youtube.com/
watch?v=EF692dBzWAs

The evolution of the computer is an interesting progression, one filled with countless technological advances, inventions, and discoveries in networking, coding, architecture, computer language, and software. One milestone in this development was IBM's introduction of the personal computer, or PC, in 1981. The personal computer had such impact that in 1982 *Time* magazine abandoned its (then-labeled) "Man of the Year" and celebrated the personal computer with its "Machine of the Year" issue. *Time* magazine publisher John Meyers discussed the selection: "Several human candidates might have represented 1982, but none symbolized the past year more richly, or will be viewed by history as more significant, than a machine: the computer" (Myers, 1983). Ironically, the feature writer produced the story on an electronic typewriter. The following year, however, *Time* would install personal computers in its newsroom.

Two years later, Apple introduced its Macintosh computer to the world with its "1984" commercial during Super Bowl XVIII. The ad is a nod to George Orwell's novel *1984*. The spot was the buzz of the country the following Monday and was featured on TV news programs and written up in the press. Anyone who didn't understand that computers were part of the new cultural fabric of America, realized it after Super Bowl XVIII.

The Internet

If you were born after 1990, you grew up using computers and the Web. Prensky (2001) would refer to you as a **digital native**, because you naturally and natively use these technologies and speak their language. You naturally and natively use the Internet several hours a day, simultaneously Facebooking, texting friends, researching a school project, and accessing just about anything from a live baseball game on ESPN to eBay. The original prototype of the Internet was developed by Rand Corporation for the U.S. military. The U.S. Department of Defense sought a secret and sophisticated communication system that could survive a nuclear attack. During its developmental stages, the government allowed access via public telephone lines to private users, primarily scientists and university researchers. Then, in 1982, the National Science Foundation refined the system and made it accessible to computer research labs. It didn't take long for digital pioneers to transmit not just words but graphics, photography, sound, and video. Their prototype, however, was still a work in progress.

The Internet would become a reality 8 years later. The man responsible was Massachusetts Institute of Technology (MIT) Professor Tim Berners-Lee (McPherson-Sammartino, 2010). He had been experimenting with networking and computer programming language. On Christmas Day of 1990, with the assistance of Robert Cailliau, Berners-Lee coordinated the first successful message transfer on the Internet. The data's content wasn't important, but creating the Internet in the process certainly was.

Media Convergence

MIT professor and computer scientist Nicholas Negroponte (Gordon, 2003) conceived the theory of media convergence and first published it. **Convergence** is a media theory that posits that previously distinct media adopt changed forms over time and merge into new ones. Negroponte further speculated that newly created media platforms alter earlier ones. For example, ereaders such as Kindle, Nook, and iPad have altered the delivery system for books we read. The Internet and multimedia presentation of the modern newspaper is another good example. Consequently, new media technologies will continue to emerge and change how we create, communicate, and process information. In other words, Negroponte maintained that convergence keeps media in a constant state of flux.

Convergence may be changing some medium or format of communication as you read this book. For example, not long ago, digital textbooks and degrees earned online were unheard of. Media are continually changing; some are dying or in the midst of a metamorphosis—works in progress, so to speak. New media are cannibalizing old media, or developing reconfigured versions of older media. In some ways, this evolving transformation is fueling technology—and vice versa. The software industry seeks faster, better, newer applications. Hardware developers are looking to find more compact and comfortable ways to stretch and strengthen electronic devices or to integrate more media or applications into a single package. For example, smartphones and tablets like the iPad are flexible, dynamic technologies that support user-created applications and that are constantly evolving in their usefulness. A newly released app can alter the way you use your device and the frequency with which you use it until the technology is transformed in some way as Negroponte predicted. It's important to realize that convergence isn't going away. Each new device or platform continues to contribute to the overall transformation Negroponte predicted. Media convergence affects commerce, culture, entertainment, socialization, economics, and communication.

Up until the late 1960s, most media stood independent from one another. Audiences had not fragmented to any great degree, and media basically stayed in their respective silos. As in Gutenberg's era, the printing press still put ink on paper and churned out newspapers, magazines, and books. Radio and television reception arrived via your antennas. The albums you bought and music you listened to were stamped in vinyl. Movie videotapes, now an outdated and obsolete form, hadn't even been introduced to consumers. Today the Internet works as a delivery system for all of these forms of expression. The Internet has simplified our lives: It has transformed how we receive and use information, how we shop, communicate with others, and obtain entertainment. We download, create, and exchange high-quality information and images faster and more efficiently than ever before.

Audience, Advertising, and the Digital Age

Ed Madison, who has worked across media for nearly 30 years, addresses some of these issues in the following interview. Madison has been a journalist and an executive producer/director of network television, film, and numerous commercial projects. Early in his career he was a founding producer for CNN, aiding in the groundbreaking quality programming that has come to represent that network. His own subsequent companies have provided services for most of the major networks and studios, including CBS, ABC, A&E, Paramount, Disney, and Discovery. In addition, Madison has contributed to the success of many top-rated series that helped to define the lifestyle/travel television genre, including *Lifestyles of the Rich & Famous, A&E Top 10*, and *Entertainment Tonight*. His present company, Engaging Media, Inc., creates, brands, and distributes high-caliber video programs and marketing messages for delivery via the Internet to mobile devices and PCs.

In a recent interview, Ed Madison talked about how he is applying and teaching storytelling via digital technologies in education. He has recently been exploring pedagogical benefits at both university and elementary levels.

The State of Media Today: Marketing and Visual Communication

Like newspapers, advertising and marketing strategies are responding to the convergence phenomenon. As Madison noted, newspapers and other media have to adjust their business models as technology and delivery platforms change and as audience migrations, attitudes, habits, and media preferences shift. One constant, however, is that visual communication and storytelling all relate in some way to business. Advertising supports most media. The number of pages in the newspapers and magazines you read is dependent upon the number of ads that are sold in those respective issues. If the advertising stalls or goes away for a publication or TV program, that magazine or TV content will go away. At the heart of all media are marketing and advertising, no matter what's being sold or where. Retailing mogul and marketing guru A. Alfred Taubaum said, "There is more similarity in the marketing challenge of selling a precious painting by Degas and a frosted mug of root beer than you thought possible" (Taubman, 2007).

Advertising finds us and markets things to us through media placement. We pay for everything from the fine art we purchase to the car we drive and the music and films we watch at home or in theaters. The same is true for the technologies and devices we use to engage visual media we consume: our TVs, gaming systems, tablets, ereaders and smartphones. Advertising follows us. Wherever we go, for whatever reason, it goes. Marketing and advertising have learning about us (and locating us) down to a science.

Along with reshaping the cultural and social landscape, the Internet has become a nexus for all media—as well as for us. In December of 2009, research results published by Harris Interactive suggested that "adult Internet users are now spending an average of 13 hours a week online. About 14% spends 24 or more hours a week online, while 20% of adult Internet users are online for only two hours or less a week." Interestingly enough, the great majority of those responding to the information were "not surprised" (Wauters, 2009). In fact, most of the comments to the survey felt that the results were underestimated.

Marketers have been gravitating to the busiest Internet sites since consumers shifted online. However, early returns for Internet advertising were not encouraging. Initial attempts at engaging the audience were initially pretty simplistic and not at all effective. Banner ads were the primary format employed. **Banner ads** are small rectangular boards usually embedded on the top or sides of a web page. The ads take advantage of interesting content through planted banner and pop-up ads. Visually, they're not very subtle or sophisticated. The banners are meant to stand out from the content and are likely to be brightly colored and exhibit movement and flash.

Advertising affiliates earn their fees through pay per click arrangements. The first banner ad was loaded on the Web for Zima malt beverage in 1994. The ad format hasn't changed much since then. Visually, they work as advertising land mines, "popping up" into view when an unsuspecting user alights on a site. Despite the fact that they've failed (typically less than 1% of them see any traffic), many advertisers continue to use them. Banner ads have proven less than effective since their inception but are still the most common advertising experienced on the Internet. Users detest them. Pop-ups are more irritating and intrusive than simple banners ads. Often the "x" or cancel-out-triggers are buried within the ad, making them difficult to exit.

Advertisers are still trying to discover an effective way to reach consumers on the Internet without alienating them. Some of the more interesting approaches have been short movies or interesting content of some kind. The latter's strategy is to engage the user in the hopes the content will be redirected virally to the original viewer's friends. The potential for advertising on the Internet is still a work in progress, but astute marketing directors have found a variety of arresting ways to integrate their brands into the digital realm. Lexus is one of those brands.

The Future of Media

The concluding section for this chapter looks at Robert Elder's vision of the future of media and visual communication in his essay "How the Future Moves." Henry Blodget, founder and editor-in-chief of *Business Insider*, concurred with much of what Elder has to say about the future. Blodget remarked, "The future of media is already here . . . all the power has shifted to digital . . . content is distantly less important than distribution" (Blodget, 2010).

Elder suggests that the future is all around us. We should all pay attention.

How the Future Moves

"I've seen the future, and it works." It's a phrase that gets attached to just about every new piece of technology that's supposed to save us time, make our lives better, and deliver us from the last piece of unwieldy technology. The line is actually a misquote from journalist Lincoln Steffens, who was talking about Soviet Russia, but since then, it has taken on a life of its own in the tech world. And the word that's most often overlooked in the phrase is *seen*. The future is visual.

Visual journalism had a rocky start on the Web, with text-minded companies building text-minded Internet experiences. But that's changed. The new wave of image- and info-based journalism has forced us to rethink our definitions of storytelling. Mobile devices, Web plug-ins and social media have not only changed journalism but also sped up its growth and expanded the skill set journalists must have. Now, in addition to video, audio, animated maps, illustrated timelines, and full-blown interactive environments, we have innovations on and mash-ups of all of the above. Information doesn't just sit in a pie graph anymore. It moves.

Take, for example, the *New York Times*' Flash graphic for the Barack Obama/Hillary Clinton Democratic primary: The shuffling blocks of data dance as the user sorts voter information by state, sex, income, and education. In the same vein, CNN.com used the map- and graph-based software Tableau to illustrate the effects of the foreclosure crisis with clickable, data-filled bubbles on a simple, elegant map. While some technologies require a new, high-end skill set, the business climate and velocity of innovation has made many of these tools cheaper and more accessible than those outside traditional journalism.

We are, as a media culture, at a crossroads. On one hand, technology has allowed for the democratization of media and journalism—look at the Arab Spring uprisings that started in 2010. On the other, more sophistication is required to parse the medium from the message. Social media tools plus advances in photo technology have broken down the barriers of whom, exactly, the messengers are. With just a few hundred dollars, almost anyone can contribute to the visual narrative as photographers, documentarians, filmmakers, music video artists, and so forth. While exciting—and important for booming business and evolving tech sectors—it's also made it increasingly difficult to break down the lines between reporting/punditry/entertainment and pure, well-crafted spin. Thus, it's important as for us as consumers to understand how journalism has changed and continues to transform from media convergence and reinvents itself.

Cutting-edge visual journalism allows more "show, don't tell"—standard advice for good storytelling—while also giving the audience insight and a simulated experience. Just because one can use the latest tools in technology, doesn't mean one always should use them.

In Hollywood, it's often said that the impressive often loses to the expressive (Orpen, 2003), suggesting that storytelling suffers amid conflicting tones, explosions, and our recent infatuation with the newest eye-popping technology. Journalists should constantly ask these questions:

- Does the message fit the medium?
- How can multimedia best serve the story?
- How can we best reach our audience?
- Is it engaging, does it tell or enhance the telling of a story?

With multimedia and visual journalism, opportunities for enhanced information transfer are greater. You can go beyond "show, don't tell" and enter the realm of experience or "simulated experience."

This was the case with the *New York Times'* basic-but-powerful game Gauging Your Distraction. Instead of offering a dry, inverted pyramid story about the perils of text messaging while driving, the *Times* built an interactive game that challenged Web readers to enter the correct toll lanes while receiving incoming texts.

Some activities/games are more sophisticated and interactive. They demand more of the user, such as the University of North Carolina's Powering a Nation: The Energy Cocktail environment. Again, with all the other tools in its storytelling arsenal, the UNC students found a way to make this activity engaging—even addictive—to explain real-world dilemmas. It's an example of journalists thinking through a business and economic lens, hoping to pass on that perspective to readers. Within that environment, they've built Balancing Act: The Energy/Water Challenge, wherein users play the part of a town manager, balancing the needs of the community and of the energy industry, all the while trying to stay in office and serve the public. It's like the board game Monopoly but with far more nuance and insight.

The next example of visual journalism will be several innovations stacked on top of old ones, with new ideas improving and challenging the old. This new breed of media includes timelines, maps, video, and audio, and creates a holistic experience. We've already seen this with Web documentaries such as Prison Valley and "Welcome to Pine Point," created by a Canadian media group The Goggles. "Welcome to Pine Point" invites users into Pine Point, a mining town that disappeared in the 1980s. Using photographs and a collage of material from Pine Point, this documentary virtually resurrects that town in a feat that mixes print journalism, video, immersive environments, and interactive elements.

Newer technologies take this even further. Using HTML 5, the band Arcade Fire and director Chris Milk built a haunting music video for "We Used to Wait," which—in almost real time—constructs an experience around the viewer's childhood home using satellite imagery and Google Maps. You can even write a note to your younger self with an electronic postcard, which is then animated into a flock of crows. Visit thewildernessdowntown.com.

The future will demand more engagement and more visual literacy from us. Technology and its developers want to know what we want to know in order to adapt and accommodate. I've seen the future, and it *moves*. But how will it move us?

References

Aspray, W., & Campbell-Kelly, M. (1997). *Computer: A history of the information machine (Sloan Technology Series)*. New York: Basic.

Barger, M. S., & White, W. B. (2000). *The daguerreotype: Nineteenth century technology and modern science.* Washington: Smithsonian.

Blodget, H. (2010). Here's the truth about the future of the media industry. *Business Insider*. Retrieved from http://www.businessinsider.com/ignition-future-of-media-2010-12

Cook, D. (2008, October 29). Monitor shifts from print to web-based strategy. *The Christian Science Monitor*. Retrieved from http://www.csmonitor.com/USA/2008/1029/p25s01-usgn.html

Cousins, M. (2006). *The story of film: A worldwide history*. New York: Thunder Mountain.

Facebook. (2012). Timeline. Retrieved from http://www.facebook.com/about/timeline

Gordon, R. (2003). Convergence defined. *USC Annenberg Journalism Review*. Retrieved from http://www.ojr.org/ojr/business/1068686368.php

Kobre, K. (2004). *Photojournalism: The professionals approach* (5th ed.). Waltham, MA: Focal Press.

McPherson-Sammartino, S. (2010). *Tim Berners-Lee: Inventor of the World Wide Web*. Breckenridge, CO: Twenty-First Century Books.

Myers, J. (1983, January 3). A letter from the publisher. *Time*. Retrieved from http://www.time.com/time/magazine/article/0,9171,953629,00.html

Phillips, W. (1884). *Speeches, lectures and letters*. New York: Lee and Shepard Publishers.

Richman, D., & James, A. (2009, March 16). Seattle P-I to publish last edition Tuesday. Retrieved from http://www.seattlepi.com/business/article/Seattle-P-I-to-publish-last-edition-Tuesday-1302597.php

Rogers, E. M. (1994). *A history of communication study: A biographical approach*. New York: Free Press.

Taubman, A. (2007). *Threshold resistance: The extraordinary career of a luxury retailing pioneer*. New York: Harper Collins.

Vogelstein, F. (2007, October 7). The Facebook revolution. *Los Angeles Times*. Retrieved from http://www.latimes.com/news/opinion/la-op-vogelstein7oct07,0,6385994.story

Wauters, R. (2009, December 23). The rumors are true: We spend more and more time online. Techcrunch. Retrieved from http://techcrunch.com/2009/12/23/harris-interactive-poll/

CHAPTER 2

Early Developments in Theory and Research

> "The general role of our media of communication in the present social order should be studied"
>
> —Paul Lazarsfeld

Given the ubiquity of mass media and the messages they provide, it is not surprising that scholars have been interested in studying mass communication. Over the last century, scholars have undertaken a number of studies aimed at determining *how* mass communication influences us, and *what* consequences that influence has.

Not surprisingly, early studies of mass communication reflected linear thinking about the way mass media operate. Accordingly, researchers focused their attention on the classic mass media—radio, television, newspapers and magazines which tended to have large, anonymous, and quite heterogeneous audiences (Wright, 1959). The thinking then was that mass media were extremely powerful forces, so much so that some scholars were "alarmed by the ubiquity and potential power of the mass media (Lazarsfeld & Merton, 1948)." One scholar at a conference expressing this perspective in the extreme stated that 'the power of radio can be compared only with the power of the atomic bomb (Lazarsfeld & Merton, 1948).' Given this way of thinking, it was natural for studies to focus on message producers and mass media in an effort to identify, in many cases, to isolate influence of the message sources, media, and messages on message receivers (Lasswell, 1960).

These studies produced a number of interesting results that advanced our understanding of mass communication's influence. Perhaps the great contribution of these studies was to heighten our understanding of the complexity of the mass communication process, and the challenges of studying it. Researchers found that it was very difficult to isolate the influence of sender, message and receiver in their studies. Moreover, it was also to isolate the influence of the entire process of mass communication from the influence of other social influences like families, friends, schools, and communities. For example, as we shall see, researchers determined that in many cases the influence that mass media and their messages had for receivers depended upon the reactions of friends, relatives, or other individuals (Katz & Lazarsfeld, 1956). While the linear model implied that media and messages had a direct influence on message receivers, researchers found that in many cases audience members were influenced by people who they looked up to—which researchers termed, *opinion leaders,* who *mediated*—came between sender and ultimate receivers in the mass communication process. This insight meant that it would be very difficult to differentiate the influence of media messages, from the influences of family, friends and other opinion leaders who helped influenced audience members' exposure to the media and their interpretation of the messages.

Over time mass communication researchers began to broaden their study of the influence process to include message consumers and the message consumption process. Accordingly, they focused attention on message receivers, and how their individual needs, attitudes, knowledge, beliefs, backgrounds, culture and social networks influenced what messages they exposed themselves to, how they interpreted those messages, and what ultimate influence these decisions had (Berlo, 1960).

This research added clarity to our understanding of the many factors and richness to our understanding of the complexity of mass communication, and also called attention to further challenges that are present in efforts to identify exactly how mass communication influences us, when that influence takes place, how particular media and messages have an influence, with whom, and with what consequence.

As mass media have grown and evolved, new, more interactive ways of thinking about how mass communication works and its impact have emerged. Traditional mass media have been joined by newer media such as cable and the internet which often cater to smaller, less diverse, and sometimes less anonymous audiences. These new media of mass communication cater to audiences that are described as *demassified.*

The audiences of media receivers for some newer media are more selective and as a group, they are sometimes less heterogenous. In the case of radio, for example many talk radio programs appeal to groups with particular political orientations—either Republican or Democratic, conservative or liberal. In so doing, such programming provide information to these groups that helps inform them, but often in a way that supports, reinforces, and validates the particular points of view, values, and biases that audience members bring to the listening experience. These outcomes occur with great regularity with many internet websites and blogs that attract individuals with similar needs, perspectives, or goals.

As media continue to evolve and become increasingly demassified, the typical approaches to thinking about and studying the effects of traditional mass media are evolving—and newer ways of thinking about and studying influence are emerging. These approaches will benefit an understanding of the complex and interactive relationship that exists between messages senders, media and consumers.

Pioneers in Media Research

Pioneering researchers from the early 20th century created theories that laid the groundwork for much of how we conceptualize the effects of media today. Charles Horton Cooley was one of the first social psychologists to establish such theories on the effects of mass media. In works such as *Human Nature and Social Order* (1902) and *Social Organization* (1909), Cooley attempted to explain the role of communication in society. In his studies, Cooley unveiled two opposing ideas. On one hand, Cooley saw new media as a way to encourage individuality by supporting ideas and customs that follow a person's self-interest. For example, if a person has political views that are not popular in his or her community, media can introduce that person to other like-minded individuals and give validation to unique ideas. On the other hand, new media limit the distribution of new ideas and customs, therefore leading to assimilation. For example, the type of language used in a widely distributed newspaper may, over time, become accepted as the universal dialect for a region, and all local dialects may disappear. Cooley explained that people have an innate desire to be alike and new media gives people information on how others talk, dress, and feel.

Cooley solved his paradox by determining that there are two different kinds of people: those who embrace isolation and those drawn to choice. Additionally, Cooley felt modern media foster isolation and obliterate choice. In other words, media will gradually eliminate the things that make us unique as individuals, communities, races, and nations. This process creates a universal understanding that although individuals may look, dress, or behave differently, we are all still extremely similar. For example, by watching a television show with homosexual characters such as *Will & Grace*, viewers can learn that homosexuals deal with the same life issues as heterosexuals. This type of effect can have a positive impact on society, as it promotes tolerance and acceptance. However, it can also have a negative effect. Since we learn about such a large variety of people, we only have the capacity to develop a superficial understanding and concern for other people. We are unable to learn about others in detail because we are overloaded with information (Downing, McQuail & Wartella, 2004). Therefore, while a syndicated sitcom may help heterosexuals learn to view gay men and lesbians as equals, heterosexuals may never take the time to learn about the personal and political issues such as gay rights that are important to the gay community. Cooley's theories were mostly based on the effects of print media. However, his studies inspired other researchers as new types of media emerged.

The Start of Extensive Study

During the 1920's the motion picture industry propelled itself into American culture. With the introduction of full length feature films like Charlie Chaplin's *The Kid* (1921) and *The Gold Rush* (1925), viewing a movie at a local theater became a common pastime for adults and children. The experience of sitting in a theater and watching a movie was like no other media at the time. Unlike newspapers and books, which only appeal to one sense, the movie-going experience activated multiple senses. The growing popularity of motion pictures caused the Motion Picture Research Council to question the amount of influence this new medium was having on audiences. This concern prompted one of the largest research projects ever conducted in an effort to understand the relationship between a medium and a specific audience. Established in 1928, the Payne Fund Studies was a series of 13 studies conducted to examine the various aspects of potential effects of motion pictures on individuals, specifically children. The studies were funded by grants from the Payne Fund and were executed by some of the most well-know social scientists of the day. The Payne Fund Studies focused on children because at the time millions of children were frequently attending movies—typically more than one a week. The Saturday matinee was a fun and inexpensive form of entertainment for young boys and girls, as many families did not have radios or televisions in their homes at the time.

Each of the Payne Fund studies was developed to address a specific question. To determine the type of content displayed in motion pictures, qualitative analysis of 1500 movies, produced between 1920 and 1930, was used to place movies in specific categories of content. Ten categories were established: children, history, comedy, crime, love, sex, mystery, travel, war, and social propaganda. The results showed over three-fourths of films dealt with only three thematic categories—crime, sex, and love. A majority of films also displayed the use of tobacco and liquor (materials that were illegal during the period of prohibition). To determine who was viewing this content, census and survey data was used to identify the ages and sex of individuals attending movies (Jowett, Jarvie & Fuller, 1996).

Well-known educator Edgar Dale studied the movie attendances of over 50 Ohio communities to estimate the size and composition of the audiences. He used this information to project estimates for the entire nation. Dale found that children five to eight years were attending movies on a regular basis and school-age children were frequent moviegoers—attending more movies per week than adults. Dale also determined that boys attended more often than girls (Lowery & DeFleur, 1995).

Once researchers understood the type of content involved in motion pictures and who was exposed to it, the next step was to determine if audiences actually retain the information embedded in motion picture content. Over three years, nearly 3,000 children and adults were tested on various types of information presented in films. They found that even children as young as eight years old acquired a substantial number of ideas from movies. In fact, retention rates were high among all age groups. Subjects were tested at six weeks and again at three months after seeing the films. In some cases, subjects tested six months after seeing the films showed even higher levels of retention. This supported the concept of the **sleeper effect**—the idea that information can sit dormant in our subconscious and emerge over time. Investigators concluded that movies provided a special learning format that caused an unusually high retention of factual information when compared to the acquisition of facts in standard laboratory experiments.

One of the more sophisticated investigations in the Payne Fund Studies involved the process of determining whether these retained ideas create an emotional response. Researchers used laboratory studies to first measure the emotional levels of a group of children before the group viewed a series of films. The children's emotional levels were then measured after they viewed the films. Researchers' tests found that most children displayed emotional responses such as anger, fear, sadness, and excitement after viewing the movies. The studies determined that the increase in emotional responses was directly related to the content in the viewed films. Meaning, motion pictures create an emotional response in children.

The most challenging part of the Payne Fund Studies was determining whether motion pictures caused children to act on their increased emotions. Through extensive study, researchers found that children who frequently attended movies also demonstrated declining morals, delinquent behavior, lower intelligence, and a number of other factors. These results lead to a complex question: does frequent movie attendance lead to unsophisticated behavior or do unsophisticated children go frequently to the movies? Unfortunately, the authors of the studies were unable to answer the question. They concluded that there was no simple cause-and-effect relationship between movie attendance and delinquent behavior. They did determine that there is a reciprocal relationship—movies do have an effect on children, but the children that are most likely to attend the most violent and aggressive movies are also most likely to participate in delinquent behavior.

While the Payne Fund Studies were unable to find definitive answers to all of the questions the studies posed, the series of studies did make the groundbreaking discovery that adults and children learn from media and that what they learn affects how they live their lives. This discovery changed the way the academic community viewed communication and new media. A number of the Payne Fund studies documented effects that would be restudied in research on other forms of media such as radio and television in later decades.

Listen: 1938 Broadcast of **The War of the Worlds**

http://www.youtube.com/watch?v=Xs0K4ApWl4g

The War of the Worlds

By the time the Payne Fund Studies published its findings on the effects of motion pictures, a new form of media was being examined. During the 1930s radio became an increasingly popular outlet for news and entertainment for American families. Millions of listeners tuned in each evening to hear news reports and radio programs. In 1938, one particular radio program changed the way social psychologists viewed media's influence over human behavior. On October 30, the CBS radio aired an episode of *The Mercury Theater of the Air* in which theater director Orson Welles adapted HG Wells's classic science-fiction novel *The War of the Worlds.* The novel's plot involved the invasion of Martians and the destruction of major cities. To condense the novel into a one-hour radio broadcast, much of the introduction was told through fictional news bulletins that "interrupted" regularly scheduled programs.

About 12 million listeners tuned in for the show; however, some listeners were not aware the program was fictional. The production value for Welles' broadcast was top-notch for the time. It had excellent special effects, professional actors, and realistic dialog, and in turn, caused many uninformed listeners to believe the invasion was real. They evacuated their homes, flooded police stations with concerned calls, and spread alarm among friends and family members. Reality eventually sank in after a few hours, and the radio network came under heavy attack. CBS issued an apology for the program. Soon after, the Federal Communications Commission (FCC) published guidelines against the practice of mixing fictional stories and news information. During the weeks following Welles' broadcast, press stories described numerous accounts of terror among listeners. While the exact number of people involved in this mass hysteria is unclear, it is estimated that as many as 6 million people believed Martians were invading the planet at the time of the broadcast.

Rethinking the Panic
• • • • • • • • • • • • • • •

http://www.slate.com/
articles/arts/history/
2013/10/orson_welles_
war_of_the_worlds_
panic_myth_the_
infamous_radio_
broadcast_did.html

The confusion that *The War of the Worlds* created was a dramatic demonstration of the power of radio. Hadley Cantril and a group of fellow broadcast researchers at Princeton University were compelled to understand what caused so many people to panic when the circumstances of the report were so unlikely to take place. Through interviews and observation, the group attempted to identify the individual characteristics that caused a person to panic or not to panic. This was the first time communication researchers describe the types of people and the types of conditions that lead to panic. While Cantril's early studies supported the idea that individuals with a low level of education were most likely to believe the broadcast was real, his later studies revealed the phenomenon was more about a person's suggestibility than education. The characteristics of high suggestibility were found to be a lack of self-confidence, a sense of fatalism, a tremendous amount of personal worry, and strong religious beliefs. While these characteristics alone do not explain a listener's reaction to the radio program, together they identify the individuals most likely to perceive the broadcast as a critical situation and are therefore more susceptible to panic (Cantril & Gaudet, 1940).

All-powerful Media

Cantril's conceptualization of media effects focused primarily on the psychology rather than the sociological aspects of the relationship between the media and society. During the early stages of media research (1900 to 1940) many thought media were a powerful force and could directly affect the views and behaviors of the public. Political scientist and communication theorist Harold Lasswell formed the analogy of the hypodermic needle off of this belief. The hypodermic needle model suggests that media can "inject" the public with whatever thoughts and opinions the media manipulators want inscribed (Glynn, Herbst, OKeefe & Shapiro, 1999). The concept is far-fetched by today's standards, but at the time the direct access media had to the public was new and unfamiliar. For the first time, messages could enter people's homes and workplaces and release information that was unfiltered by human interaction.

Because researchers felt the public was highly susceptible to the influence of media, they attributed the Nazis' gain of power to the extensive and intelligent use of radio, film, and print media. In Germany during the 1930s, the Nazi political party used posters, pamphlets, and radio programs to promote the party's ideas and agenda. Mass communication played an important role in both World War I and World War II, as many nations, including the United States, used political propaganda—widely distributed pieces of communication used to harness support for political objectives—to encourage patriotism among one's own country or hatred for an enemy. Lasswell published many works on the subject of propaganda and politics, and was eventually given the task of organizing the Wartime Communication Study for the United States Library of Congress. He became famous for posing the question "who says what in which channel to whom with what effect?" in his studies (Mattelart, Mattelart, Cohen & Taponier, 1998). This question, which was essentially a formula, prompted researchers to examine the various facets of media effects research instead of focusing on how one thing affects another.

Media as Limited Power

After the end of both world wars, communication researchers began to change their views on the power of media. New types of studies demonstrated that media did not have as much influence over society's actions and opinions as a whole as previously thought. During the 1940s, Austria-born American sociologist Paul Felix Lazarsfeld and his colleagues at Columbia University pioneered the use of scientific surveys to understand the influence of mass media on public opinion. He was interested in examining the impact of newspapers, magazines, radio, and motion pictures on the voting habits of Americans. Lazarsfeld conducted a large-scale study that used statistical information to gauge the change in the public's views. Initially Lazarsfeld thought that exposure to mass media messages could sway a voter's decision. However, the results of his study determined that media had little effect on voter's opinions. He found that political party affiliation was far more influential than media content. While most voters followed the campaigns through media sources, they gave most of their attention to the content that supported their political affiliation.

This concept gave rise to the selective perception theory. The selective perception theory states that individuals respond and perceive media messages differently, based mostly on their own personal needs and interests. Instead of affecting groups the same way, the effects of media messages would be personalized, depending on what people *selected* to retain. This process of selective recall was basically in place to gratify the individual needs of each audience member.

> ### The Public Opinion Quarterly
>
> The American Association of Public Opinion Research (AAPOR) was founded in 1947 by a group of researchers interested in understanding the public's response to media. The organization was founded under the idea that if we can develop a better understanding of how the public feels, we can develop and implement programs that promote peaceful living. The AAPOR developed the *Public Opinion Quarterly*, which became an official journal in 1948. It was the first university journal on mass communication. Leading researchers such as Harold D. Lasswell, George H. Gallup, and Paul F. Lazarsfeld were central to the advancement of the AAPOR and the history public opinion research. (American Association for Public Opinion Research, History, n.d.)

Later, Lazarsfeld joined forces with researcher Elihu Katz and used the selective perception theory to develop the uses and gratifications theory, which placed even greater influence on personal needs and individual uses of the media to define how messages affected audiences. As the name implies, uses and gratifications theory places great emphasis on the personal gratification each individual gets from the media to explain why and how we select the messages we consume and how those messages affect us (Ball-Rokeach, 1998).

Lazarsfeld and Katz's findings helped them develop the two-step theory. This theory proposed that media messages first influenced economic and political power elites, or opinion leaders, who later propagated them through interpersonal contact or by using the media themselves. Thus, instead of directly affecting the masses, messages were first processed by opinion leaders, who gave them their own spin before they were disseminated to a larger public. Popular in the 1950s and 1960s, this theory lost some of its power once media channels multiplied and popular access to this multitude of channels became more of a reality (Ball-Rokeach, 1998).

The Technological School

In addition to theories suggesting that mass communication products have a *direct* effect on consumers, there are others proposing that this influence is significant but *indirect*. One such group of theorists has focused its research efforts on the impact of the media themselves rather than on the messages they convey. These researchers have been termed the "medium theorists," and together form what could be called *the technological school*. Proponents of the technological school do not dismiss the idea that particular messages may have various effects on particular individuals, audiences, or behaviors. They contend, however, that the most substantial impact of mass communication lies in the more general and indirect effects of different communication technologies (including writing, printing, and electronic media) on modes of thought, patterns of human interaction, and the structure of societal institutions. Because of its origins, this line of thought is sometimes also called the Toronto School.

This emphasis can be summed up by the saying that "the medium is the message." Marshall McLuhan, author of this memorable phrase, was one of the earliest, and certainly the most widely known, of the medium theorists, and he and his mentor, Harold Innis, did much to highlight this point of view. Innis argued that Western culture has been deeply influenced by the spatial bias and cognitive processes associated with print media, which he believed has promoted cultural complexity, but also confusion and alienation.

McLuhan shared with Innis the conviction that communication media are extensions of the human mind and body. He considered modern electronic media to be a sort of extension of the human nervous system, an extension that circles the globe and establishes a network of interpersonal involvements that he referred to as a "global village," an aphorism that has been widely used to describe the Internet, which was adopted and popularized only decades after McLuhan coined that emblematic phrase.

Joshua Meyrowitz and Manuel Castells are other thinkers who have made major contributions to the technological school of thought in media effects. Meyrowitz's book *No Sense of Place* (1985) examines the influence of electronic media on the construction of particular kinds of cultural environments in which our roles and behavior patterns are played out. In Castells' massive three-volume book *The Information Age* (1997), Castells deals with the social, political, economic, and cultural impact of the so-called information society on our daily lives. In the trilogy's second volume

"The Power of Identity," he focuses particularly on how new media and new technologies are changing the ways in which we organize and define ourselves.

A Modern Look at Media Effects

Towards the end of the 20th century, some researchers started to look at media effects from a new angle. They began to examine not just how the public is affected by the media, but how the pubic *thinks* they are affected by the media. Born in the early 1980s, the third-person effects hypothesis states that people tend to believe media messages influence others more than themselves. It claims that as audience members, we resist the idea that we can be directly affected by messages, and instead tend to believe that other people are always more influenced than we are. This hypothesis is still very favored in mass communication research, and many studies have been published that tend to confirm it. Born out of the third-person effects hypothesis, a more recent model, called the indirect-effects model states that people tend to perceive the effect that media messages have on others and then react to their perception. For example, we would hear so much about a popular show such as *Dancing with the Stars* or *American Idol*, that even if we are not fans we would assume that those shows are very influential on audiences, and might be tempted to "jump on the bandwagon" so that we won't be left out.

Important Issues in Media Effects

In psychological theory, social learning involves learning behavior that is controlled by environmental influences rather than by inherent or internal forces. Modeling is a typical result of social learning. Modeling is a type of learning that occurs when an individuals observes the actions of others to gain information on how to behave. You probably participate in modeling on a daily basis. In class you may notice your peers diligently taking notes. Regardless of whether or not you use class notes to study, you may start taking notes simply because it seems like appropriate behavior for the setting. While it seems bizarre, many of the choices you make every day are based on modeling the behavior of others rather than making an internal decision. For example, you look out the window of your home and notice that most people outside are wearing jackets. Without going outside to test the temperature for yourself, you decide that since everyone is wearing jackets it must be cold and you put on a jacket before leaving the house as well.

Bandura's Bobo Doll

In 1961, Albert Bandura conducted an experiment to study the effects of viewing violence on children. Bandura used 36 boys and 36 girls enrolled at Stanford University Nursery School whose ages ranged from 3 to 5 years old. The subjects were divided into eight experimental groups and 24 subjects were put into a control group. The experimental groups were shown a video that displayed an adult model hitting, throwing, and kicking an inflatable doll called a Bobo doll, as well as using aggressive language. After viewing the video, the children were left in a room by themselves with the same BoBo doll and other toys. The children were told all of the toys were there for them to play with. The study showed that the majority of the children who were exposed to the aggressive video played with the Bobo doll and repeated much of the same violent behavior and language displayed in the video. Other parts of Bandura's study showed that the Bobo doll video encouraged some subjects to participate in other aggressive acts such as gun play and harsh language (Bandura, Ross & Ross, 1961).

Children are active participants in modeling. American psychologist Albert Bandura was one of the pioneers of modeling theories. He conducted numerous studies showing that when children observe the actions of others they learn many forms of conduct. Behaviors such as sharing, aggression, cooperation, social interaction, and disappointment are picked up from the individuals in their environment.

Bandura Explaining the Bobo Doll Experiment

http://www.youtube
.com/watch?v=
Pr0OTCVtHbU&
feature=youtu.be

Violence

Bandura's insights into the learning habits of children led him and many other psychologists to question the effects of the media, specifically television, on the behavior of children. If children learn to be aggressive or introverted from the people in their environment, it is possible that they can learn similar behavior from the people on their television set (Encyclopedia Britannica, 2008). Research on the effects of violence in the media has been controversial. Two types of theories have been proposed. One suggests that a child's urge to participate in violent behavior can be diverted by watching violent behavior on television. In other words witnessing violence lessens the drive to commit violence. Under this theory, a young girl who watches a cartoon character play a violent prank on another character will be less likely to play a violent prank on a classmate. The second theory suggests that viewing violent behavior actually increases the drive to participate in violent activities. Following Bandura's idea of modeling, children model their behavior after the images they see on TV. Under this theory, the same little girl that witnessed the prank simulated in a cartoon would be more likely to initiate a similar prank on a classmate.

Violence in the media, especially on television, has been a concern since the medium became popular, in the 1950s. A great deal of effects research has focused on violence in the media, where researchers have gone back and forth between a more critical position, which says that media violence has a great influence on causing aggressive behavior on consumers; and a "limited effects" position, which is still concerned with the impact of violent messages but sees their influence as more moderate.

In the late 1960s two governmental commissions—the National Commission on the Causes and Prevention of Violence, and the Surgeon General's Scientific Advisory Committee on Television and Social Behavior—undertook a series of research studies. On the basis of laboratory experiments and field studies, the Surgeon General's committee concluded, somewhat cautiously, that viewing violence on television contributes to violent or aggressive behavior in viewers. Just how much this influence really amounts to is still a point of disagreement for specialists. In general, most studies have supported that there is a causal relationship between watching violent programming and acting aggressively.

In the past 15 years, the discussion about violence in the media has gained even more strength on the basis of the popularity of video games and hip-hop music. In the early 1990s, Congress once again focused its attention on violent rap lyrics, denouncing artists such as Ice-T for what they saw as the aggression and incitement contained in lyrics for rap songs such as "Cop Killer." In the late 1990s, the attention shifted to the violence in video games. Incidents such as the Columbine and Arkansas school shootings led parents, educators, and other groups to argue that the extreme violence contained in some video games was influencing children to behave more aggressively.

Several states have passed laws that ban the rental or sale of violent video games to minors, and the Supreme Court in 2010 will consider whether the California version of this law violates the Constitution.

Violence in the media is a compelling and contentious subject for both consumers and researchers. Some feel the media is often used as a scapegoat for other causes of violence in our society. It is often easier to blame a popular video game for an increase in firearm-related deaths than blame the government's policy on gun control. Still no person can deny that there is a substantial amount of violence in the media today. The average child under the age of 14 is exposed to 11,000 murders on television in his/her lifetime (Chandler, 2004). According to The National Television Violence Study, nearly two out of three TV programs contained some violence, and average about 6 violent acts per hour (The Kaiser Family Foundation, 2003).

Many theories have been developed to explain the various effects of mediated violence on audiences. The catharsis theory claims media outlets such as television can ease children's urges to participate in violent behavior. According to the theory, mediated violence allows aggressive people to discharge their anger vicariously through the media images, therefore lessening aggressive behavior. The concept of the catharsis theory dates back to Aristotle and the ancient Greeks. In his work *Politics*, Aristotle stated that viewing tragic plays allows people to release emotions related to negative feelings such as grief, rage, and fear.

Other theories of media effects claim that media change society's perception of violence. Television is often used to express the collective stories of our culture. From the life of spoiled high school students in California to the gritty intricacies of the judicial system, many television shows, whether fact or fiction, attempt to interpret a cultural story. The cultivation theory views television as a main source of storytelling for heavy viewers (those who watch more than four hours of television a day). Because these viewers look to television instead of their own experiences to shape their views of the world, their beliefs about society are warped and often less favorable than reality. This theory grew out of the work done by George Gerbner and his colleagues in the Annenberg School of Communications at the University of Pennsylvania. Since the late 1960s, Gerbner and his group have measured the amount of violence in prime-time television programming and tried to correlate that to the perception that television viewers hold about "real-life" violence. Gerbner associates this altered perception with mean world syndrome, a condition in which a person interprets the world as a far more dangerous place than it is in reality. For example, individuals who watch numerous hours of dramatic entertainment such as *CSI: Miami* or *Law & Order* may feel that the murder rate in this country is much higher than it is in reality. By producing a yearly Violence Profile, the group, also known as the Cultural Indicators Project, tries to establish a causal link between watching television and how we perceive reality.

Cultivation theory proposes that in the long term, television "cultivates" or shapes the way in which we see the world, creating a homogenous and fearful society. Findings from this research tend to support the view that the more television (or violent programming) people watch, the more distorted their perception of the real world or real-life violence will be.

A study done by the American Academy of Pediatrics focused its attention on violent video games, noting that the most popular video games tend to have "behavioral scripts" in which players not only are rewarded for their violent actions, but also learn to act in a way that goes from choosing a violent scenario to resolving that conflict through the use of violence. Video games have been accused of encouraging children and young teens to commit real-life crimes, and in some cases they are used as a form of defense in court.

While the judicial system is not ready to accept violent video games as the primary cause of violent behavior, many professionals are. David Walsh, a child psychologist, believes that exposure to violent video games can cause teenagers to participate in violent behavior. He supports his beliefs with research conducted by the National Institutes of Health, which shows the brains of teenagers are not fully developed. According to Walsh, the impulse control center of the brain, the section that helps us think ahead, control urges, and consider consequences, is under construction during the teenage years. When this low level of control is combined with a continuous flow of violent images, Walsh believes teenagers are capable of violent behavior without fully understanding the consequences. Walsh admits that other risk factors such as a troubled upbringing can contribute to violent behavior, but violent video games heighten the impulses of those troubled teenagers (CBS News, 2005).

A more recent study focused on violent images in music videos, especially music videos made available online by cable channels such as MTV, BET, VH1, and Country.com. The study found that 185 out of 951 videos analyzed (16.4%) contained acts of violence. Although the proportion found was relatively low, the author of the article was troubled by the kind of violence portrayed, where 76% of all violent acts were assisted by the use of weapons. The study also found that hard rock (72% of videos) and hip-hop/rap (48% of videos) were the musical genres where violence was more often committed.

The vast majority of studies analyzing violence in the media point toward three general areas of concern:

1. **Increased levels of aggressiveness.** Children and teenagers, especially boys, who are exposed to heavy levels of media violence, tend to perceive real-life violence as the natural, accepted way to resolve conflicts. Most of these children also tend to act more aggressively when they are playing or having other types of social interaction.

2. **"Mean world" syndrome.** A steady diet of violent media over a long period of time tends to cultivate in users the perception that the real world is a "mean and violent" place, which might lead to feelings of anxiety, alienation, and depression.

3. **Desensitization.** Refers to the widely tested hypothesis that constant exposure to violent messages might lead to a loss of sympathy for victims, less proactive involvement in preventing/stopping violence, and a general perception of violence as a normal occurrence.

Sex and Pornography

The production and consumption of sexually explicit material such as books, magazines, and videos is a worldwide business of enormous dimensions. The Internet and other digital technologies such as DVDs added new ways to make pornographic material even more widespread and accessible. But while many consumers enjoy a regular diet of such material, others find it distasteful, obscene or corrupting.

With a wide range of views concerning what is offensive and what is not, what is pornographic and what is simply erotic, what has artistic merit and what does not, it is obviously difficult to formulate definitions or a widely accepted concept of obscenity. Even the courts have a very hard time determining clear limits or legal concepts that could be applied across the board.

Such concerns have led Congress to dedicate a whole section of the Telecommunications Act of 1996 to the issue of pornography on the Internet. The courts have subsequently struck down some of these rules as unconstitutional and in conflict with the protections warranted by the First Amendment.

Despite the legal ramifications, the discussion rages on about the potential harmful effects of pornographic messages in the mass media. Research on the functions and effects of sexually explicit material in the media began in earnest with the establishment in 1970 of the Presidential Commission on Obscenity and Pornography. Since that time a good deal of study has been done on the various aspects of this issue, including the influence of pornography on the image and treatment of women and on the relationship between the sexes, on the physiological effects of viewing such material, and on the possible relationship between pornography and violent crimes such as rape and murder and other forms of aggressive behavior.

More recently, a great deal of criticism has focused on the depiction of women on hip-hop lyrics and music videos. Many feminists and other media critics have argued that those lyrics and videos often degrade women and present them as subservient to men. Others have focused their attention on popular video games, which they accuse of objectifying and stimulating violence and aggressive behavior toward women, many times presented in a very sexual manner.

Analyses of the content of pornographic materials have provided some evidence that messages of the supremacy of men over women are often present. Other research indicates that viewing pornography can contribute to attitudes of increased acceptance of violence toward women. Other studies, however, show that sexually explicit material portraying men and women as partners or equals can educate and help to reduce antisocial attitudes. Although some studies indicate a relationship between high rates of availability and/or consumption of pornography and high rates of rape, a causal relationship has never been found, so it would be premature to say, on the basis of this research, whether, or how, one causes the other.

A study done recently showed that 83% of the most popular TV shows among teenagers in 2001–2002 had sexual content, while on average each hour of programming contained 6.7 scenes with sexual references. In the same study, only 1% of shows containing sexual behavior focused on the risks or negative aspects of it, while only 3% of scenes analyzed discussed sexually transmitted diseases or pregnancy. A similar study argues that exposure to high dosages of sexual content might not only stimulate sexual behavior in children, but also artificially age them, accelerating their developmental stages and making children act between 9 and 17 months older than their actual age.

Ethics and Antisocial Behavior

Other concerns with potentially harmful effects of media come from those who worry that some messages might be eroding traditional ethical values, thus stimulating antisocial behavior. Some media critics argue that negative media messages are so pervasive that they might be creating a sense of alienation and frustration in younger generations, manifested in a disregard for commonly accepted cultural traditions and societal rules, and leading to apathy, cynicism and nihilism. Religious leaders often raise similar concerns.

Other critics note that pervasive and widespread media use might lead to a society that places excessive importance on materialism, appearances, and the consumption of material goods. These critics see the preponderance of commercial media messages as an indication that mass communication has lost its power to educate and socialize, or at least that younger generations are being socialized into a community that sees them only as potential buyers. Many media literacy programs have been developed and adopted by educators concerned with these potentially harmful media effects.

Stereotypes

In general, research suggests that media messages tend to reflect and perpetuate gender and ethnic stereotypes, for example. Scientists want to know how much of these stereotypes affect our perception of reality. Many of the men and women characters appearing on television present somewhat stereotyped male and female images. Various studies have shown that children, who are heavy television viewers, when asked whether certain activities or occupations would be associated with women or with men, gave answers more in line with television stereotypes than did lighter viewers.

Research also indicates, however, that programs with characters in atypical occupational roles can educate children away from the traditional sexual stereotypes. Additionally, it has been found that boys almost always choose male characters as ideal role models, and that girls sometimes choose female characters but also often choose male ones.

A similar situation happens with ethnic stereotypes. Content analyses of television programming have shown the lack of ethnic diversity on mainstream television programs, as well as the presence of harmful ethnic stereotypes, or yet the association of particular ethnicities with certain occupations. Studies have shown that people who are heavy television viewers, or who rely heavily on television for information about the world, tend to associate some ethnic minorities to stereotypical behaviors presented on television.

Education and Socialization

Questions concerning the educational, cultural or social impact of mass media have been discussed and debated for centuries. In ancient Greece, Plato warned that writing weakens the mind and destroys the memory. In the fifteenth century, similar complaints were leveled against printing, though many people defended it as an unprecedented means for distributing and increasing knowledge. From the birth of electronic media on, the focus has been on television.

Studies have shown that people who spend a great deal of time watching television have lower Intelligence Quotients or IQs than people who spend less time doing so. However, more recent studies have shown that children who spend a limited amount of time watching television (two hours per day, on average), actually perform better academically than children who do not watch TV at all. It is uncertain from both sets of studies if there is a causal relationship between television viewing and intellectual performance. Our understanding of the relationship between reading behavior and TV viewing also remains uncertain. Some studies have found a positive correlation over time among younger viewers, while other studies have shown that adults who spend no time reading watch much more television than those who read. Similarly, the nature of the connection between viewing and both academic performance and educational aspiration has not yet been unraveled; so many factors—such as grade level, gender, television content, and type of school subject—seem to be implicated in this complex relationship.

On the positive side, researchers have also studied the effects of so-called educational programming, such as *Sesame Street*, and found that not only the content of these programs can help children strengthen certain cognitive abilities such as problem solving, reasoning, language, and arithmetic skills, but also that the form or style of presentation can stimulate the development of other important mental operations. The research also suggests that the educational impact of television viewing is affected by the nature of the family and social relationships prevailing in the child's environment.

Quite a bit of media research has examined the ways in which people, including children, use communication messages in the socialization process. Researchers have investigated the influence of media such as television, music, movies, and videogames on the development of personal identity and on the association of certain attitudes and behavior patterns with particular sexes, ages, races, and occupations. If so much of what we know about the world comes from the media, researchers are interested in finding out how much impact the content of these messages have on the socialization process, our personalities, and the development of our worldviews.

References

American Association for Public Opinion Research, History. (n.d.). Retrieved from http://windowsxp-privacy.net/?id=198760161

Ball-Rokeach, S. (1998). A theory of media power and a theory of media use: Different stories, questions and ways of thinking. *Mass Communication and Society, 1*(1/2), 5–40 (referencing the work of Katz and Lazarsfeld).

Bandura, A., Ross, D., & Ross, S. A. (1961). Bandura: Transmission of aggression through imitation of aggressive models. *Journal of Abnormal and Social Psychology, 63*, 575–582.

Berlo, D. (1960). *The process of communication: An introduction to theory and practice.* New York: Holt, Rinehart and Winston.

Cantril, H., & Gaudet, H. (1940). *The invasion from Mars: A study in the psychology of panic.* Princeton: Princeton University Press.

CBS News. (2005). Can a video game lead to murder? *CBS News,* March 6, 2005. Retrieved from http://www.cbsnews.com/stories/2005/ 03/04/60minutes/main678261.shtml

CBS News. (2003). AP, "Teen charged in Alabama cops shooting." *CBS News,* June 9, 2003. Retrieved from http://www.cbsnews.com/stories/2003/06/07/national/main557477.shtml

Chandler, D. (2004). Television violence and children's behavior. Retrieved from http://www.aber.ac.uk/media/Modules/TF33120/tv-violence_and_kids.html

Downing, J., McQuail, D., & Wartella, E. (2004). *The SAGE handbook of media studies,* Thousand Oaks: California.

Encyclopedia Britannica. (2008). Social learning. *Encyclopedia Britannica.* Retrieved from http://www.britannica.com/EBchecked/topic/551304/social-learning

Glynn, C. J., Herbst, S., OKeefe, G. J., & Shapiro, R. (1999). *Public opinion.* Boulder, CO: Westview Press.

Jowett, G. S., Jarvie, I. C., & Fuller, K. H. (1996). *Children and the movies: Media influence and the Payne fund controversy.* Cambridge: Cambridge Press.

Katz, E., & Lazarsfeld, P. F. (1956). *Personal influence: The part played by people in the flow of mass communications.* New York: Free Press.

Lasswell, H. D. (1960). The structure and function of communication in society. In L. Bryson (Ed.), *Communication of ideas* (pp. 117–130). Champaign, IL: University of Illinois Press.

Lazarsfeld, P. F., & Merton, R. K. (1948). Mass communication, popular taste, and organized social action. In L. Bryson (Ed.), *The communication of ideas.* Reprinted in Peters J. D., & Simonson, P. (Eds.). (2004). *Mass communication and American social thought: Key texts 1919–1969,* (p. 230). Lanham, MD: Rowland and Littlefield.

Lowery, S., & DeFleur, M. L. (1995). *Milestones in mass communication research: Media effects.* USA: Longman Publishers.

Mattelart, A., Mattelart, M., Cohen, J. A., & Taponier, S. G. (1998). *Theories of communication.* Thousand Oaks, CA: Sage Publishing.

The Kaiser Family Foundation. (2003). *Key facts, Spring 2003.* Retrieved from http://www.kff.org/entmedia/upload/Key-Facts-TV-Violence.pdf

Wright, C. (1959). *Mass communication: A sociological perspective.* New York: Random House.

CHAPTER 3

Evolution of Media Theory

> "All around us are the consequences of the most significant technological, and hence cultural, revolution in generations"
>
> —*Lawrence Lessig*

Mass Communication in Contemporary Society

Contemporary society maintains a reciprocal, interdependent relationship with the mass media. Society influences the media and is itself influenced by mass or mediated communication. Rarely a day goes by without some mention of how the media and mass communication affect our lives. Newspaper and radio reports scream headlines such as, "Studies link teen suicides with TV news and movies," "Kids, TV Don't Mix," and "Music videos found to be less violent than prime-time TV." Through mass media, people learn almost immediately about major happenings across town or across the globe. As viewers, we are frequently eyewitnesses to global events both joyous and tragic.

Definitions and conceptualizations of mass media and mass communication have changed considerably over the last decade. At one time, not too long ago, mass media was defined primarily as radio, television, newspapers, and magazines. Today, the term *media* is likely to conjure terms such as *cable* and *satellite television, satellite radio, HD radio,* and *interactive media,* also referred to as computer-mediated communication (CMC). Some even include the cell phone as a form of mediated communication (Noll, 2007, p. 1). Indeed, "the idea of 'new media' captures both the development of unique forms of digital media, and the remaking of more traditional media forms to adopt and adapt to the new media technologies" (Flew, 2002, p. 11). That is, new media combines computing and information technology, communications networks, and digitized media and information content. There are a few fundamental differences between what has been termed "new media" and traditional media. The new mediated technologies allow the user to communicate in a two-way fashion with others. In the past, after reading a story in a print newspaper, you had an opportunity to write a letter to the editor and send that via conventional (or snail) mail. Today, after reading the same story on the Internet-based version of the news source, you can send immediate feedback to the source via e-mail. This immediacy factor represents another major difference. Putting a print newspaper or magazine together takes an enormous amount of time. Adding a story to a news Internet site, often complete with video, reduces that time frame considerably.

One consequence of these innovations and of the changing nature of media use has been the development of new theories of mass communication. These theories attempt to explain how individuals respond to media, to predict how rapidly a society will adopt these innovations, and to determine what effect mass communication has on individuals, society, other forms of human communication, and culture. Current research looks at the role of society, culture, and the individual in the *production* of mass communication content. The distinction between mass communication and interpersonal communication has stimulated a considerable amount of investigation by communication researchers. Some theories address how mass communication and interpersonal communication *jointly* influence an individual's decision-making processes. Other theories attempt to offer a new synthesis of interpersonal and mass communication, which has been labeled *mediated interpersonal communication.* Three broad questions have stimulated much of the research and theory building in mass communication:

1. What is the impact of a society on its mass media?
2. How does mass communication function?
3. What effect does exposure to mass communication have on people?

The bulk of mass communication theory and research has concentrated on the third question. Many theorists have investigated how mass media messages affect people's perceptions and behaviors. Examples of those theories will be detailed in this chapter. Some of the theories explore audience involvement in mass communication. Other theories try to explain how mediated messages shape our perceptions of reality. Yet another body of research examines how communication rules are used to guide audience members' collective interaction with mass media.

The reflective-projective theory of mass communication asserts that the mass media act like mirrors for society. The media reflect society's attitudes and values as they simultaneously project idealized visions of a society. Individuals interpret these reflections, seeing both their own images and alter-native realities. Interpretations are affected by the intellectual, emotional, and sensory responsiveness of each individual. Lee Loevinger (1979) argued that nations or communities are not necessarily formed by maps or geographical boundaries. Rather, nations or communities are formed by common images and visions, along with common interests, ideas, and culture.

A Closer Look at the Magic Bullet Theory

http://www.youtube
.com/watch?v=
Qt5MjBlvGcY

Early Theory-Building Efforts in Mass Communication

During World War I, the new mass media were used to help activate the population. The mass media presented messages designed to stimulate support for the war effort. The newly developed media effectively promoted the beliefs of the warring nations. Mass communication became an important tool used by individuals engaged in large-scale persuasive efforts. The term *propaganda* first emerged during this time. After World War I, U.S. society witnessed an increasing growth in diversity; the society became less homogeneous. Individuals were no longer so closely dependent on one another. The term "mass society" was created by sociologists to describe not merely a large number of people in a given culture but the *relationship* between the individuals and the social order around them (DeFleur & Ball-Rokeach, 1982).

The Magic Bullet Theory

Sometimes referred to as the "hypodermic needle theory," the magic bullet theory was one of the first developed to explain the influence of the new forms of communication on society. The bullet theory and the many variations of it were derived from the stimulus-response perspective of several early mass communication theorists and researchers (e.g., Lasswell, 1927). This view asserts that any powerful stimulus such as a mass media message can provoke a uniform response from a given organism, such as an audience. Recall that the mass media at this time were thought to exert powerful, direct influence over the audience. The magic bullet or hypodermic needle theory suggested that the mass media could influence a very large group of people *directly* and *uniformly* by "shooting" or "injecting" them with appropriate messages designed to trigger a desired response.

The popularity of these early stimulus-response theories of mass communication was consistent with that of the existing psychological and sociological theories of mass society. In addition, "evidence" of the power of the media existed in its ability to mobilize support for the country's war effort. The newly emerging mass media did have a profound effect on the audience, but several intervening factors also exerted considerable influence on audiences during that time. After years of additional research, mass communication theorists concluded that the early stimulus-response theories lacked explanatory and predictive power. They developed alternative theories that address both the power of the media to influence attitudes and behavior and also the influence of different message sources and different audience reactions. Examples of these alternative theories will be presented later in this chapter.

The Two-Step Flow Theory

Several researchers had designed a study to examine how individuals from different social groups select and use mass communication messages to influence votes (see Lazarsfeld, Berelson, & Gaudet, 1944). The researchers expected to find empirical support for the direct influence of media messages on voting intentions. They were surprised to discover, however, that *informal, personal contacts* were mentioned far more frequently than exposure to radio or newspaper as sources of influence on voting behavior. When questioned further, several participants revealed that they had received their information about the campaign *first* from *others* (who had received information directly from the mass media).

Armed with this data, Elihu Katz and Paul Lazarsfeld (1955) developed the two-step flow theory of mass communication. This theory asserts that information from the media moves in two distinct stages. First, individuals who pay close attention (are frequent "attenders") to the mass media and its messages receive the information. These individuals, called opinion leaders, are generally well-informed people who pass information along to others through informal, interpersonal communication. Opinion leaders also pass on their own interpretations in addition to the actual media content. The term "personal influence" was coined to refer to the process intervening between the media's direct message and the audience's ultimate reaction to that message. Over the last fifty years, a substantial amount of research has contributed to our knowledge about opinion leadership.

Several characteristics of opinion leaders have been identified. Opinion leaders are quite influential in getting people to change their attitudes and behaviors and are quite similar to those they influence. Think of an individual whom you consult before making a major purchase. Perhaps you have a friend who knows a great deal about cars. You may hear a number of messages on television about the favorable qualities of the Ford Fusion and the Toyota Camry. The mass media have clearly provided you with information about each car, but do you rely solely on this information to decide which car to buy? If you are like most people, probably not. You may check *Consumer Reports* to determine what it says about those two cars. Will this information be enough to persuade you to prefer one car to the other? Possibly, but chances are you will also seek out the advice of someone you consider an opinion leader on the topic of automobiles.

The two-step flow theory has improved our understanding of how the mass media influence decision making. The theory refined our ability to predict the influence of media messages on audience behavior, and it helped explain why certain media campaigns may have failed to alter audience attitudes and behavior. Despite this contribution, the two-step flow theory has also received its share of criticism. First, some major news stories seem to be spread directly by the media with only modest intervention by personal contact. Acts of terrorism or natural disasters are often heard first from the media, then discussed interpersonally. Second, definitions of opinion leadership are often vague. Werner Severin and James Tankard (2001) suggested that some opinion leaders are self-nominated and are not reported to be opinion leaders by their supposed followers. Another difficulty is that opinion leaders have been found to be both active and passive. The two-step flow theory argues that opinion leaders are primarily active media seekers, whereas their followers are primarily passive information "sponges." This distinction between media behavior of leaders and followers does not necessarily hold true. Finally, although Katz and Lazarsfeld argued the need for a *two-step* model, the process of media dissemination and audience behavior can involve more steps. Thus, the two-step flow theory gave way to the concept of multistep flow, often used to describe the *diffusion of innovations.*

Diffusion Theory

Diffusion theory examines how new ideas spread among groups of people. The two-step flow theory of mass communication was primarily concerned with the exchange of information between the media and others. Diffusion research goes one step further. It centers around the conditions that increase or decrease the likelihood that a new idea, product, or practice will be adopted by members of a given culture. Diffusion research has focused on five elements: (1) the *characteristics of an innovation* that may influence its adoption; (2) the *decision-making process* that occurs when individuals consider adopting a new idea, product or practice; (3) the *characteristics of individuals* that make them likely to adopt an innovation; (4) the *consequences* for individuals and society of adopting an innovation; and (5) *communication channels* used in the adoption process (see Rogers, 1995).

Communication channels include both the mass media and interpersonal contacts. The multistep flow and diffusion theories expand the number and type of intermediaries between the media and the audience's decision making. In multistep diffusion research, opinion leaders still exert influence on audience behavior via their personal contact, but additional intermediaries called change agents and gatekeepers are also included in the process of diffusion. Change agents are those professionals who encourage opinion leaders to adopt or reject an innovation. Gatekeepers are individuals who control the flow of information to a given group of people. Whereas opinion leaders are usually quite similar to their followers, change agents are usually more educated and of higher status than either the opinion leaders or their followers. A change agent might be a representative from a national cable television company who tries to persuade local opinion leaders in a community (town officials, for example) to offer cable television or a computer company representative who convinces local school officials to introduce a particular personal computer into the school system. This representative is probably more knowledgeable about the computer system than the opinion leaders (school officials). However, the task of influencing the school board to budget money still rests with the local opinion leaders. Recall that opinion leaders are similar to those they represent. Previous research (see Chapter 9) suggests that similarity or homophily enhances attraction, liking, and influence. A gatekeeper might be the editor of a local news show or newspaper. This person decides what stories will be printed or broadcast. Gatekeepers represent yet another intermediate step in the flow of information between the media and audience. Thus, a number of intermediaries and channels are involved in the process of information dissemination and influence.

Early theory-building efforts in mass communication relied heavily on psychological and sociological theories. The field of mass communication now has produced theory that can "stand on its own." Several contemporary theories developed by communication scholars will be presented next. The first theory, the functional approach, was based on the early research and continues to be refined today.

The Functional Approach to Mass Communication Theory

The mass media and mass communication serve many functions for our society. Clearly, one of the main attractions is escapism and entertainment value. We come home after a hard day at school or the office and turn on our favorite television comedy, game show, or dramatic program. Another major use of the media is to provide information. Driving to school or work, we turn on the radio and catch the latest news, weather, and sports scores. We may listen to our favorite talk program to hear what others think about relations between the United States and China. Harold Lasswell (1948) articulated three functions of mass communication: *surveillance, correlation,* and *cultural transmission.* Charles Wright (1960) added a fourth function, *entertainment.* In 1984, Denis McQuail added a fifth function: *mobilization.*

Surveillance refers to the information and news-providing function of mass communication. When we turn on the radio to obtain the latest weather, traffic, or stock market reports, we are using the media primarily for its surveillance function. When the stock market dropped 508 points on October 19, 1987, millions of Americans turned on their radio and television sets to obtain information about the plunge. In every major office in the country that day, workers were "glued" to their radios to discover how much their companies' stocks had fallen. Individuals who did not own stock read in-depth reports in local newspapers concerning the potential influence of the stock market crash on the national and global economies.

The second function, correlation, deals with how the mass media select, interpret, and criticize the information they present to the public. The editorials on radio and television and the persuasive campaigns waged using the media are primary examples of the correlation function. "USA for Africa," "Live Aid," "Farm Aid," and "Hands Across America" were campaigns whose origins and major fund-raising drives were stimulated by and developed in connection with the media. The outpouring of funds to help the starving people of Ethiopia was largely stimulated by the poignant images that came into our homes via television. Many political critics suggest that the media, and not the American people, select our political leaders. They point to the tremendous media coverage and scrutiny given to the private lives of politicians and media celebrities as an example of the correlation function of the media. Along with criticism and selection of events, the correlation function of the media also *confers status* on selected individuals. The mass media choose to highlight a number of individuals who then become "legitimized" to audiences.

The third function, cultural transmission, refers to the media's ability to communicate norms, rules, and values of a society. These values may be transmitted from one generation to another or from the society to its newcomers. Cultural transmission is a teaching function of the media, which brings many social role models into the home. Those role models frequently engage in behaviors considered appropriate in a given society (prosocial behaviors). Johnston and Ettema (1986) cited shows such as *Mister Rogers' Neighborhood, Sesame Street,* and the *ABC After School Specials* as examples of children's programs that attempt to teach or to promote such prosocial behaviors as being polite, dealing with anger or fear, handling new situations, coping with death, persisting at tasks, caring, and cooperating. Prime-time television shows such as *Brothers and Sisters* and *Friday Night Lights* have been mentioned as programs that promote values such as respect for authority, family harmony, and a solid work ethic. As the number of television hours watched increases, regional and subcultural differences appear to be decreasing. The media's powerful cultural transmission of "common" messages has caused us to speak, think, and dress more alike. These common or unifying messages may have further "homogenized" U.S. culture by dictating the "proper" way to act.

The fourth function of mass communication, entertainment, may be the most potent one. Mass communication helps fill our leisure time by presenting messages filled with comedy, drama, tragedy, play, and performance. The entertainment function of mass communication offers an escape from daily problems and concerns. The media introduce us to aspects of culture, art, music, and dance that otherwise might not be available to us. The mass media can stimulate excitement in viewers (as with sporting events) or calm us (as with classical music broadcasts). Mass communication as entertainment provides relief from boredom, stimulates our emotions, fills our leisure time, keeps us company, and exposes us to images, experiences, and events that we could not attend in person. Numerous critics, however, assert that the media and its messages lower expectations and reduce fine art to pop art.

McQuail's fifth function of mass communication, mobilization, refers to the ability of the media to promote national interests (as we saw in the discussion about World War I), especially during times of national crisis. Although this mobilization function may be especially important in developing nations and societies, it can occur anywhere. We may have seen evidence of it in the United States during the days after the assassination of President John F. Kennedy and during the coverage of the terrorist attacks of 9/11. The media's central function was not only to inform us but also to counsel, strengthen, and pull us together.

Agenda-Setting Theory and Mass Communication

Agenda setting describes a very powerful influence of the media—the ability to tell us what issues are important. For example, if the media choose to highlight declining wages and lower standards of living for the current generation of adults, then concern over the economy becomes an important issue, regardless of the level of importance we placed on it before the media attention. Books addressing the issue start to sell across the country. Suddenly, people are concerned about loss of leisure time compared to previous generations. Entertainers joke about children in their thirties moving home to live with their parents.

Agenda setting has been the subject of attention from media analysts and critics for years. As far back as 1922, the newspaper columnist Walter Lippman was concerned that the media had the power to present images to the public. Because firsthand experiences are limited, we depend on the media to describe important events we have not personally witnessed. The media provide information about "the world outside"; we use that information to form "pictures in our heads" (Lippman, 1922). Political scientist Bernard Cohen (1963) warned that "the press may not be successful much of the time in telling people what to think, but it is stunningly successful in telling its readers what to think about." Prior to the early 1970s, the prevailing beliefs of mass communication research were that the media had only limited effects. Most research assumed the following sequence: the media generate awareness of issues through presentation of information; that information provides a basis for attitude change; the change in attitude includes behavior change. Most research looked for attitude and behavior change and found very limited influence. A study by Max McCombs and Donald Shaw (1972) in Chapel Hill, North Carolina, changed the emphasis of research efforts and stimulated a flurry of empirical investigations into the agenda-setting function of the mass media.

McCombs and Shaw focused on awareness and information. Investigating the agenda-setting function of the mass media in the 1968 presidential campaign, they attempted to assess the relationship between what voters in one community *said* were important issues and the *actual* content of media messages used during the campaign. They first analyzed the content presented by four local papers, the *New York Times*, two national newsmagazines, and two national network television broadcasts. They ranked importance by looking at the prominence given a story (lead, frontpage, headline, editorial, etc.) and the length. The researchers then interviewed 100 undecided voters (the assumption being that voters committed to a candidate would be less susceptible to media influence). McCombs and Shaw concluded that the mass media exerted a significant influence on what voters considered to be the major issues of the campaign. In addition to pioneering an entire line of research, McCombs and Shaw provided an excellent example of the thinking on which this textbook is premised. They believe that effective scientific research builds on previous studies. As a result, their study of the next presidential election (Shaw & McCombs, 1977) extended the scope of the original study, the objectives, and the research strategies. The study took place in Charlotte, North Carolina, and extended the analysis over time using a panel design. One of the interesting objectives added to this study was the investigation of what types of voters would be more likely to depend on the media. The researchers looked at two factors—the relevance of information to an individual and the degree of uncertainty—in determining need for orientation. Voters with a high need for orientation would be more likely to be influenced by the media in determining the importance of issues when issues were relevant and uncertainty was high. Just as McCombs and Shaw expanded their focus, other researchers have extended investigations of agenda setting to issues including history, advertising, foreign, and medical news.

Despite the extensive outgrowth from the original hypothesis, critics charge that there is insufficient evidence to show a causal connection between the order of importance placed on issues by the media and the significance attached to those issues by the public. McQuail (1984, p. 276) argued that, at least for the time being, agenda-setting theory remains "within the status of a plausible but unproven idea." The direction of influence still needs to be resolved. Do the media influence the opinions of the audience or reflect public concerns? Are both dictated by actual events? Do external or internal forces have more influence on media content? What roles do the elite media play? That is, if the *New York Times* runs a story, can the *Washington Post* afford to ignore it? How much power do special interest groups, the president, senators, or chief executive officers of large corporations have to pressure the media to present their views? Is credibility a balancing factor? The media are in business; does profit and loss play a larger role than a culture that prides itself on presenting unbiased reports? Other research could look at internal processes. What effects do deadlines, space restrictions, and the use of official sources have? The number of variables offer new opportunities for research on this topic for years to come.

Mass Communication and Parasocial Interaction

The influence of mass communication and the media extends into the domain of relationship development. The concept of parasocial interaction has received considerable attention from both mass communication and interpersonal communication theorists. The concept was introduced forty years ago by Horton and Wohl (1956) to describe a new type of "relationship" that exists between television viewers and remote media communicators. In a parasocial relationship, members of the audience view performers or the characters they portray as belonging to the audience's peer group. Media performers with whom audiences develop parasocial relationships include entertainers, talk show hosts, journalists, sport personalities, and a number of other national and local media personalities.

We often develop a sense of involvement with media performers. We follow their careers just as we follow the careers of actual friends and colleagues. We may look forward to reading Internet, newspaper, and magazine accounts of their lives. We may even go to great lengths to meet them. One of your authors, for example, is a fan of "talk radio" programs. For years, he listened to TalkNet radio celebrity Bruce Williams give advice to listeners on a variety of topics. When visiting other cities, the author would scan the dial to locate the nationally syndicated program. This gave the feeling of having the performer "travel with him" and made it seem that he had a "friend," even in the most distant city. Bruce Williams scheduled a local appearance at a very large ballroom; the author immediately purchased tickets. Convinced that he would be among only a small audience on a wintry evening, the author arrived only fifteen minutes before the event was to begin. He was amazed to discover a capacity crowd, with only a few seats left in the very back of the ballroom! Clearly, he had underestimated the number of people who had also developed a parasocial interactional relationship with this particular radio celebrity.

In parasocial interaction, viewers believe that they know and understand the media personality in the same way as they know and understand their "real" friends (Perse & Rubin, 1989). The parasocial relationship is based on the belief that the media performer is similar to other people in their circle of friends (Rubin, Perse, & Powell, 1985). For most audience members, these parasocial interactions augment their actual face-to-face relationships.

In another study, researchers hypothesized that viewers would regard their favorite media performer as "closer" to them than actual "acquaintances" but more distant than "friends." Because most of our interpersonal relationships can be classified as "acquaintanceships," this hypothesis projected that we place our favorite media personality as "closer" to us than many people with whom we interact. Results showed that television personalities hold an intermediate position in "closeness" between friends and acquaintances. Koenig and Lessan (1985) suggested that the term *quasi-friend* may be most appropriate in describing the relationship between viewer and television personality.

Levy (1979) reported that news viewers occasionally reply to a newscaster's opening greeting with a greeting of their own. Almost 70 percent of network news viewers said they noticed when their anchorperson was on vacation, and 25 percent of viewers indicated that the anchorperson's absence "upset" them (p. 72). Levy also portrayed parasocial interactions as an alternative to face-to-face relationships for some people who have few or weak social ties with other people. A report by the American Psychological Association's Task Force on Television and Society reported that the elderly watch television more than any other age group. For this group in particular, as well as for other isolated individuals, television viewing becomes a parasocial activity that helps create the illusion of living in a world surrounded by people. Parasocial relationships with media personalities often fill the "gaps" caused by the death of a spouse or by children leaving home. Alan Rubin and Rebecca Rubin (1985) argued that "it is possible and beneficial to see media in certain contexts as being functional alternatives to interpersonal communication" (p. 38).

Uses and Gratifications Theory

As director of the Office of Radio Research at Columbia University, Paul Lazarsfeld published the first work on uses and gratifications (Lazarsfeld & Stanton, 1944). One of his former students, Herta Herzog, worked extensively on a program of research on daytime radio serials. She investigated the characteristics of women who listened to serials, the uses they made of the information they listened to, and the gratifications they received from their choice of programming (Lowery & De Fleur, 1995). The perspective that resulted from this early research presented a direct challenge to the powerful effects conceptualization of the magic bullet theory.

The next major study from this perspective was by Schramm, Lyle and Parker (1961). They conducted eleven studies from 1958 through 1960 on how children used television. The emphasis was on the choices of programming children made to satisfy their needs and interests. After these pioneering efforts, numerous studies have mined this vein of research. Uses and gratifications theory attempts to explain the *uses* and *functions* of the media for individuals, groups, and society in general; it represents a *systems approach* that uses covering laws methods of investigation.

One tenet of the systems approach is that a change in one part of the system will, of necessity, cause a change in another part of the system. Many claim that DVRs, DVDs, and TiVo have altered television viewing patterns. For example, recording television programs allows people to fast forward through the commercials. As a consequence, advertisers and advertising agencies have reexamined the placement and the format of commercials shown during network programming. Earlier we looked at the five functions of mass communication in terms of the *content* of mass media. The emphasis on content implies a passive audience absorbing what is offered. Uses and gratifications research changed the emphasis to audience members as active participants selecting particular forms of media.

Objectives of the Theory

Communication theorists had three objectives in developing uses and gratifications research. First, they hoped to explain *how* individuals use mass communication to gratify their needs. They attempted to answer the question: *What* do people do with the media (A. Rubin, 1985)? A second objective was to discover the *underlying motives* for individuals' media use. *Why* does one person rush home (or stay up late at night) to watch the local news on television while another person prefers reading the newspaper during breakfast or after dinner, while another prefers to get news only from the Internet? Why do some people only watch HBO movies? These are some questions that uses and gratifications theorists attempt to answer in their research. A third objective of this line of theory building was to identify the positive and negative *consequences* of individual media use. Here the systems aspect of uses and gratifications theory emerges. Relationships between the individual and the mass media, media content, the social system, alternative channels of communication (such as friends), and the consequences of media choice are all avenues of inquiry for systems researchers.

Examples of Uses and Gratifications Research

At the core of uses and gratifications theory lies the assumption that audience members actively seek out the mass media to satisfy individual needs. For example, Rubin (1979) uncovered six reasons why children and adolescents use television: learning, passing time, companionship, to forget or escape, excitement or arousal, and relaxation. Television viewing for passing time, for arousal, and for relaxation emerged as the most important uses of television for this age group. Rubin also designed a questionnaire called the Television Viewing Motives Instrument to discover reasons why people watch television.

Rubin (1983) designed another study to explore adult viewers' motivations, behaviors, attitudes, and patterns of interaction. The study looked at whether TV user motivations could predict behavioral and attitudinal con-sequences of television use. Five primary television viewing motivations were examined: pass time/habit, information, entertainment, companionship, and escape. The strongest viewing motivation relationships were found between pass time/habit and both companionship and escape viewing. The two categories of viewers identified in this study were predecessors to the *ritualized* and *instrumental* users of television discussed next. The first group of viewers used television to pass time and out of habit. The second group used television to seek information or as a learning tool.

Rubin (1984) identified two types of television viewers. The first type (habitual) consists of people who watch television for ritualized use. This type has a high regard for television in general, is a frequent user, and uses television primarily as a diversion. The second type (nonhabitual) consists of people who attend to television for instrumental use. This type exhibits a natural liking for a particular television program or programs and uses media content primarily for information. This person is more selective and goal oriented when watching television and does not necessarily feel that television is important. Rubin argued that ritualized television use represents a more important viewing experience for the audience member, whereas instrumental television use represents a more involving experience for the viewer.

In a study of Swedish television users, Levy and Windahl (1984) identified three types of audience activity. The first, called *preactivity*, is practiced by individuals who deliberately seek certain media to gratify intellectual needs. For example, some viewers deliberately select newscasts to be informed about current events. The second type, *duractivity*, deals with the degree of psychological attentiveness or involvement audience members exhibit during a television viewing experience. The focus is on how individuals interpret and decipher mediated messages. The comprehension, organization, and structuring of media messages leads to certain intellectual and emotional gratifications for viewers. For example, trying to figure out the plot or ending of a dramatic program on television is one example of the duractivity use of the media. The third type of audience activity, *postactivity*, deals with audience behavior and message use after exposure to mediated messages. People involved in postactivity attend to a mediated message because they feel the information may have some personal or interpersonal value. Individuals who actively seek out television news to provide content for interpersonal communication such as "small talk" exhibit postactivity audience behavior.

Another assumption of uses and gratifications theory is that audiences use the media to fulfill expectations. For example, you may watch a science fiction program such as *Star Trek* to fantasize about the future.

A third assumption of uses and gratifications theory is that audience members are aware of and can state their motives for using mass communication. In Levy and Windahl's study, participants were able to describe how particular media gratified certain needs. The researchers found that the primary motivation for watching TV news was to gain information about the world, rather than for diversion. Studies that investigate how individuals use the media for gratification primarily employ *self-report measures*, questionnaires that ask participants about their motives for using the mass media. The television viewing motives instrument is one such questionnaire.

One study addressed several social and psychological factors associated with patterns of audience media use. Donohew, Palmgreen, and Rayburn (1987) tested a random sample of subscribers to cable television. Through telephone and mailed questionnaires, they collected demographic (age, sex, income, education, marital status) and lifestyle information. Participants also provided information on their social, political, economic, cultural, and communication-related behaviors. The researchers asked questions about the need for stimulation, gratifications sought from cable TV, satisfaction with cable TV offerings, number of hours of cable TV viewing per day, and number of newspapers and magazines subscribed to by the respondents. Four lifestyle types emerged. Type I was labeled the disengaged homemaker. This individual was primarily female, middle-aged, lower in education and income and used the media for companionship and to pass the time rather than for information or arousal. According to Rubin's classifications, the disengaged homemaker appears to represent the *ritualized* media user. The second type of individual, the outgoing activist, was also frequently female, somewhat younger, well-educated, had a good income, and was less likely to be married. Outgoing activists were highest in need for stimulation among the four types. They enjoyed staying informed and were primarily print media users. They did not watch a great amount of television and were least gratified by cable TV. Donohew, Palmgreen, and Rayburn speculated that type II's active lifestyle leaves them little time for television viewing. The third type of individual was labeled the restrained activist. These individuals were older and had the highest educational levels. More than half were female, and they were likely to be married and to have relatively high incomes. They had low need for sensation but high need for intellectual stimulation. They exhibited strong informational needs and viewed themselves as opinion leaders. They were heavy users of both print media and television, especially for informational purposes. Their media use patterns follow those of Rubin's *instrumental* user. The final type of user identified was called the working class climber. This person was primarily male, lower in education and income, and middle-aged; most were married. Working class climbers were ambitious and self-confident. They did not engage in an activist lifestyle and ranked low in need for intellectual stimulation. They were highest among the four types on television exposure and satisfaction with cable TV. They were quite low on print media usage. According to Rubin's taxonomy, they would be classified more as ritualized than as instrumental media users. The results of this study helped clarify our understanding of the many lifestyle variables that influence mass media use.

Criticisms of the Theory

Since its inception, uses and gratifications theory has enjoyed widespread popularity among mass communication theorists, researchers, and practitioners. The theory has also received its share of criticism. Much of the criticism points to an insufficient theoretical basis, particularly in defining key concepts. Alan Rubin (1985) argued that there are too many different meanings associated with the terms "audience motives," "uses," and "gratifications," which has slowed unified theoretical development in this area.

The research has been criticized on methodological grounds. Self-report questionnaires have typically been used in uses and gratifications studies; the *reliability* and *validity* of self-report data have been questioned. Some critics believe that individuals cannot respond accurately to questions about their own feelings and behavior. For example, researchers often identify the "needs" of participants through questions asked about why they use the media (Severin & Tankard, 2001). The self-reported answers about motive may be suspect or the categories assigned by the researcher may be questioned as to whether they are scientifically verifiable. If respondents cannot supply reasons when asked open-ended questions but quickly select answers from a list provided by the researcher, are those answers reliable and valid?

Even contributors to this body of research find problems with its scope. Blumler (1979) and Windahl (1981) suggested that uses and gratifications does not represent a single theory. They call uses and gratifications an umbrella concept in which several theories reside. McQuail (1984) argued that scholars have tried to do too much—trying to link the identity and attributes of audiences with the behavior traits of individuals and the role of the media in society plus the cultural origins of the patterns and meanings sought by users and producers. He suggests that the research should be more limited in scope and should take a cultural-empirical approach to how people choose from the abundance of cultural products available.

Other critics find that the theory pays too much attention to the individual without looking at the social context and the role of media in that social structure. This lack of a unified theory has led to misuse of the empirical method of inquiry. Alan Rubin (1985) suggested that audience motive research based on this theory has been too compartmentalized within particular cultures or demographic groups. This has thwarted synthesis and integration of research results, activities critical to theory building.

Cultivation Theory

The cultivation theory of mass communication effects was developed by George Gerbner and his associates at the Annenberg School of Communication at the University of Pennsylvania. The theory has been tested by numerous empirical studies. Cultivation theory asserts that television influences our view of reality. A causal relationship is suggested between television viewing and perceptions of reality—thus situating the theory in the law-governed approach to mass communication. Cultivation theory (Gerbner, Gross, Morgan, & Signorielli, 1980, 1986) asserts that television is primarily responsible for our perceptions of day-to-day norms and reality. Establishing a culture's norms and values was once the role of formal religion and other social initiations. Previously the family, schools, and churches communicated standardized roles and behaviors, serving the function of enculturation. Television now serves that function. It has become the major cultural transmitter for today's society (Gerbner & Gross, 1976a, 1976b). "Living" in the world of television cultivates a particular view of reality. Some argue that television provides an experience that is more alive, more real, and more vivid than anything we can expect to experience in real life!

The Interaction of Media and Reality

One of the authors read an article in a local newspaper that illustrates the tendency to confuse a real event with images absorbed from television. A reporter had stopped his car at the intersection of a rural road and a larger highway. He noticed a car speeding on the highway at approximately 100 miles per hour. As the car reached the point where the reporter was stopped, it suddenly tried to make a left turn without slowing down. It clipped a light pole and flipped over on its back, wheels still spinning. No one else was in sight. The reporter described staring forward, not believing what he had just seen. He recalled his mind saying to him very clearly, "What you are seeing isn't real, You are just watching a movie." For almost ten seconds he just sat there, waiting to see what would happen next. Of course, nothing happened, and he realized that it was up to him to help. He fell prey to two fears as he approached the car—one artificial (induced by previous television images) and one very real (which contradicted other images received). Television portrayals of overturned cars invariably end with fires and explosions. With televised accidents, no "real man" thinks twice about rushing to a scene where someone may be dead or horribly mutilated. The reporter was very afraid on both counts. Television is so pervasive that the line between illusion and reality is blurred. We sometimes mistake a real event for a televised one; we probably make the opposite mistake more frequently. This phenomenon provided the basis of the research into cultivation theory.

Heavy versus Light Television Viewers

George Gerbner's participation in two national studies provided the foundation for cultivation theory. He contributed a content analysis of television programming to the National Commission on the Causes and Prevention of Violence in 1967 and 1968 and for the Surgeon General's Scientific Advisory Committee on Television and Social Behavior in 1972. Gerbner and his colleagues tracked the incidents of violence portrayed during a randomly selected week of fall prime-time programming plus children's weekend programming. They compiled the percentage of programs marked by violence, the number of violent acts, and the number of characters involved in those acts. They found violent acts portrayed in 80% of prime-time programming; children's shows were the most violent of all. Older people, children, women and minorities were the most frequent victims—despite the fact that three quarters of characters portrayed on television were white middle-class males.

Building on this work, the researchers surveyed viewers to determine the number of hours spent watching television daily, the programs selected and why, attitudes about the probability of being a victim of crime, perceptions about the numbers of law enforcement officials, and general attitudes about trusting other people. Gerbner and his associates classified people as heavy viewers (four or more hours daily) and light viewers (two hours daily or less).

Cultivation theory predicted that heavy viewers would perceive the world as more dangerous because of repeated exposure to violent television portrayals. Persistent images of danger and violence color views of reality and create the perception of a mean world. Heavy viewers overestimated their chances of being involved in a violent crime. They also overestimated the number of law enforcement workers in society.

Individuals frequently confuse media-constructed reality with actual reality. Gerbner and Gross (1976b) reported that in the first 5 years of its broadcast life, the television show *Marcus Welby, M.D.*

(a fictional doctor portrayed by Robert Young), received over a quarter of a million letters from viewers. Most of the letters contained requests for medical advice! Television is highly effective in the cultivation process because many of us never personally experience some aspects of reality but the pervasive presence of television—constantly available for relatively little expense—provides a steady stream of mediated reality. We may have limited opportunities to observe the internal workings of a real police station, hospital operating room, or municipal courtroom. Thus, the media images become our standards for reality. Have you noticed that the New Year's Eve parties we actually attend *never* seem quite as exciting as the New Year's Eve parties we see on television?

The theory predicted uniform effects for all heavy viewers—regardless of factors such as gender, education, socioeconomic group, or media preferences (for example, reading newspapers versus viewing televised newscasts). As the primary source of socialization, television's messages provide a symbolic environment that transcends demographic differences. The only factor that seemed to have an independent effect on perceptions was age. Respondents under thirty consistently reported that their responses were more influenced by television than those of people over thirty (Gerbner & Gross, 1976b). Because people thirty and under have been "weaned" on television, the influence of media messages may be especially potent.

Refinement of Cultivation Theory

In response to criticisms that cultivation theory ignored the contributions of other variables (see next section), Gerbner and his associates introduced the factors of mainstreaming and resonance (Gerbner, Gross, Morgan, & Signorielli, 1980). Mainstreaming refers to the power of television to present uniform images. Commercial sponsors want to appeal to the broadest possible range of consumers, so television presents mainstream images. Differences are edited out to present a blended, homogenous image acceptable to a majority of viewers. Differences in perceptions of reality due to demographic and social factors are diminished or negated by the images projected on television. Ritualistic patterns reinforce sameness and uniformity. Resonance describes the intensified effect on the audience when what people see on television is what they have experienced in life. This double dose of the televised message amplifies the cultivation effect.

Criticisms of the Theory

Despite the large data set supporting the theory, the cultivation effect has encountered several challenges. Hughes (1980) reanalyzed data used in the original research and failed to support the core assumptions of cultivation theory. He suggested that the measures of heavy viewing only relate to total exposure to television, not specifically to what is watched. Certain personality characteristics related to the selection of television programs were not controlled in the earlier studies. He also reported that television may actually cultivate realistic and functional perceptions of the world. Hirsch (1980) found that if other variables are controlled simultaneously, very little effect remains that can be attributed to television. In his review of the original data, he found that even people who did not watch television perceived the world as violent and dangerous.

Conversely, it has been argued that major assumptions of cultivation theory may be correct, but the procedures used to study it may be incapable of uncovering the effect. Hawkins and Pingree (1982) reviewed 48 research studies conducted on the cultivation effect. They concluded that modest evidence supports the influence of television viewing on perceptions of reality. In fact, covering laws researchers find fault with the admission by Gerbner and his associates that the measurable effects of television are relatively small. Although the creators of the theory point to the cumulative effect of repeated exposure to limited influence (something like the steady drip of a faucet that eventually overflows the pail), scientific research relies on observable effects in laboratory settings that control for other influences. Cultivation researchers used self-reports of viewing habits; they did not observe respondents in a carefully controlled setting.

Potter (1986) concluded that the cultivation effect may be more complex than is currently stated; the amount of exposure to television may be less important than the attitudes and perceptions of individuals exposed. His conclusions match the criticisms from the rules perspective that fault cultivation theory with treating all viewers as helpless to withstand the manipulated images of reality projected by television. The interactions of audiences, television, and society are complex and cannot be reduced to simple cause and effect.

Cultivation theory links heavy television viewing with a distrustful view of a violent world. The final criticism questions the meaning of that link. The research has demonstrated a correlation between certain behaviors and certain attitudes, but has it proven the direction of influence? Do people who are distrustful watch more television because they have few friends? Cause and effect have not been established. There is no doubt that the controversy surrounding the media's influence on our perceptions and behavior will continue to rage. We can expect more research from scholars of mass communication in this area. New findings will refine and advance our efforts to theorize about the effects associated with the mass media.

The Spiral of Silence Theory

The spiral of silence theory was developed by Elisabeth Noelle-Neumann, a German researcher, in 1974. The theory has implications in three areas: (a) mass media and communication, (b) the individual and interpersonal communication, and (c) public opinion (Salmon & Glynn, 1996). It is considered one of the "most highly developed and one of the most researched theories in the field of public opinion" (McDonald, Glynn, Kim, & Ostman, 2001, p. 139). The theory has generated a considerable amount of research, as well as controversy, since its debut.

Contemplating the question: "Are you more or less willing to express your beliefs on an issue depending on whether you think those beliefs are widely shared by those individuals around you?" guides us to an appreciation of the theory. Noelle-Neumann's spiral of silence theory argues that individuals who think that their opinions and beliefs are not widely shared by others (in a given reference group, or in society in general) will feel pressure to express another opinion (the majority opinion) or will choose to remain silent.

According to the theory, people assess whether their opinions match those of the majority from several cues in their environment (Glynn, Hayes, & Shanahan, 1997). The media are important sources for these cues. The mass media often "serve as the representation of the dominant views in society" (Perse, 2001, p. 110) and help shape public opinion. People depend on the media as a primary source of information about social norms, customs, acceptable styles of dress and fashion, and even what to think.

Spiral of silence theory suggests that people have a fear of social isolation; that is, they do not want to be seen as different from the majority. Adolescents are especially sensitive to "fitting in" with the majority regarding the clothes they wear and the expressions they use to communicate. Noelle-Neumann believes that most people also strive to avoid social isolation by refusing to express beliefs and opinions that they feel do not enjoy majority support. To express a belief that is either "old-fashioned" or "socially unacceptable" is more than most people are willing to do (Salmon & Moh, 1992). Indeed, isolating yourself from others by expressing your true belief, when it goes against the majority view, is seen as a far worse outcome than remaining silent (Glynn, Hayes, & Shanahan, 1997). Noelle-Neumann suggested that this "spiral of silence" leads one viewpoint or one position to dominate public opinion, while others (perceived minority viewpoints) often disappear from public awareness because the people who hold less accepted views or positions remain silent. However, if people find that their opinions are widely shared by the majority or are gaining acceptance, they will be more likely to express their positions.

Some people do not succumb to the spiral of silence. Labeled "hardcores," these people do not feel the same constraints of social pressure or fear the social isolation attached to expressing minority viewpoints. Hardcores have an unusually high amount of interest in the issue; their positions remain relatively unchanged (McDonald, Glynn, Kim, & Ostman, 2001). Hardcores represent only about 15 percent of the population (Salmon & Moh, 1992).

The issue of cigarette smoking in public offers an excellent example of the effects of majority opinion on verbal (and nonverbal) behavior. For many years nonsmokers were apprehensive about speaking out against smoking in public, and the nonsmoker almost certainly did not approach smokers and request that they put out their cigarettes. In the last two decades, however, this situation appears to have changed dramatically. The nonsmoker now represents the majority opinion—that smoking has no place in public contexts (Salmon & Glynn, 1996). The reticence about criticizing smoking behavior disappeared when public opinion changed.

How did this change occur? How did the former "minority view" become the current "majority view"? The spiral of silence theory suggests that the changing messages projected by the mass media contributed greatly to the change of public opinion. According to the theory, individuals scan the environment for information about which opinions are gaining support and which are losing (Gonzenbach, King, & Jablonski, 1999). Clearly, over the last two decades the media's predominant message has been one of "antismoking." The removal of ads for cigarettes on broadcast television, the increased frequency of "public service" spots describing the dangers of smoking, and the reports in the media that fewer Americans are smoking today compared to two decades ago have helped create change. Today, the smoker is caught in the "spiral of silence" regarding expressing opinions about smoking in public. This reversal of positions is a prime illustration of a tenet of the theory: willingness to speak out changes the climate of opinion so that the dominant opinion becomes stronger. In turn, the dominant view as presented in the media yields a greater likelihood that individuals will speak up (Gonzenbach et al., 1999).

People who hold the less-dominant position will become increasingly reluctant to express their position. Their silence erodes the less-supported position even more. When the media report that adherents to a given position are criticized frequently or even physically attacked (Gonzenbach et al., 1999), they reduce the probability that individuals will voice the unfavored position. For example, when the antifur message of groups such as P.E.T.A (People for the Ethical Treatment of Animals) received more attention from the media, including reports of individuals wearing natural fur being physically attacked, individuals who previously expressed support grew more silent.

Communication studies have examined the role of the spiral of silence theory regarding a number of different issues and from several methodological perspectives to help refine and extend the theory. One study tested the spiral of silence theory that judgments about majority opinion are made through direct observation and, in particular, from television. The researchers measured both the exposure to media by individuals in the national sample and their perceptions of what position was most supported on the issue of whether homosexuals should be allowed to serve in the U.S. military. The study found that respondents with higher levels of media exposure believed that more of the public agreed with them, whereas those with low levels of media exposure perceived lack of support for their position on that issue (Gonzenbach et al., 1999, p. 290).

Spiral of silence theory was also used to test public opinion on another controversial issue: whether the United States should declare English as the official language (Lin & Salwen, 1997). The study hypothesized that an individual's willingness to speak out about this issue would be related to his or her perceived national and local public opinion. Participants in two diverse cities (Miami, FL, and Carbondale, IL) were randomly surveyed by telephone. They were asked whether they were "willing" or "unwilling" to express their opinion about this issue in public with another person who held a different opinion about the issue of making English the official language of the United States. The findings generally supported the assumptions of the spiral of silence theory. Respondents in both cities indicated greater willingness to discuss the issue in public when the media coverage of this issue was seen as generally positive or supportive (Lin & Salwen, 1997). As the national and local media coverage of this issue became more positive, younger and better-educated respondents indicated even more willingness to express their opinion on this issue (Lin & Salwen, 1997).

Some researchers have explored how the realism of the setting for the expression of public opinion might affect an individual's willingness to speak out (Scheufele, Shanahan, & Lee, 2001). Would people in a more realistic setting be less willing to present their position than those who were asked to speak out in a hypothetical situation? College students responded to questions concerning their levels of media use, their knowledge about genetically altered foods, and their attitudes toward that topic. Half of the respondents were asked if they would be willing to discuss their opinion about the topic at a hypothetical "social gathering." The other half were told that there would be a second part of the study in which they could express their opinions about genetically altered food in greater detail with other students in a focus-group interview context. The study supported a major tenet of the spiral of silence theory: fear of isolation was negatively related to people's willingness to express an opinion on genetically altered food. The data also suggested that the situation influences willingness to speak out on an issue. Respondents who were told that they would be presenting their opinions in a focus group interview context were less willing to present their opinions than those in the hypothetical "social gathering" context.

Researchers have questioned whether the "spiral of silence" effects can be observed or even studied in cultures other than Germany (Salmon & Glynn, 1996). Several researchers have challenged the methodology used in studies attempting to test the theory (Scheufele & Moy, 2000). In particular, they questioned whether the "fear of isolation" adequately explains willingness to speak out in experimental studies (Glynn & McLeod, 1985) and whether the hypothetical versus actual nature of this willingness to speak out in experimental studies may be sufficient to produce "spiral of silence" effects (Glynn, Hayes, & Shanahan, 1997). Some researchers have proposed alternative methods to measure willingness to speak out, a critical variable in spiral of silence research. Jeffres, Neuendorf, and Atkin (1999) suggested that the results of studies using the "hypothetical situation" method (where participants are asked to place themselves in a hypothetical situations and then asked how they would respond) "either have been mixed or have not supported the theory" (p. 121). Instead, these researchers obtained actual opinions and quotations both orally and in writing during interviews in shopping centers, waiting rooms, on the street, and in coffee shops, thus securing behavioral measures of willingness to express an opinion to a stranger. Another study employed a unique method to obtain the measure of "willingness to speak out." The researcher studied letters to the editor published in *Time, Newsweek,* and *U.S. News and World Report* before and after the shootings at Columbine High School to determine attitudes toward gun control (Lane, 2002).

Media Dependency Theory

Media dependency theory was developed by Sandra Ball-Rokeach and Melvin DeFleur (1976). Although Ball-Rokeach is a professor of sociology and communication, this research emerged from the communication discipline. Media dependency theory's debut was in a communication journal, and many of the articles that present extensions of this theory also appear in communication journals. Media dependency theory argues that the more dependent an individual is on the media for having his or her needs fulfilled, the more important the media will be to that person. Although some communication scholars consider media dependency theory to be an offshoot of the uses and gratifications theory of mass media, there are some differences. A major issue in uses and gratifications theory is, "*Where* do I go to gratify my needs?" whereas media dependency theory focuses on the issue, "*Why* do I go to *this* medium to fulfill *this* goal?" (Ball-Rokeach, Power, Guthrie, & Waring, 1990). Dependency theory suggests that media use is primarily influenced by societal relationships, whereas uses and gratifications theory places greater emphasis on individual media selection. Uses and gratifications theory focuses more on a person's active participation with mass media, whereas dependency theory tends to focus more on the social context in which media activity occurs. Because it emphasizes the interaction of the individual, media, and society, dependency theory uses a systems approach to studying mediated communication.

Dependency theory emphasizes the *relationship between society and the media.* There are a number of mutual dependencies. The media rely on government for legislation to protect media assets and for access to political information. The political systems of a society rely on the media to reinforce political values and norms, to help mobilize citizens to vote, and to inspire active involvement in political campaigns. Society depends on the media for the creation of information, advertising, and technology that it uses (Rubin & Windahl, 1986). The commercial broadcasting system of the United States, for example, is built on dependency between the media, advertisers, and audiences. Television programs are produced to attract large audiences so that advertisers can sell their products and services to those audiences. The media then depend on this advertising revenue to stay in business. Each system depends on the other.

The *relationship between the media and the audience* is crucial as well, for it influences how people use mass media. Audiences may depend on the media for information, for escape, and for "information" on what is considered appropriate or normative behavior. Television programs that emphasize prosocial messages such as honesty and morality are designed to teach acceptable behavior in our society.

The *relationship between society and the audience* examines how society influences the audience and vice versa. Society depends on audiences because individuals who comprise a society are seen as potential voters, potential consumers, and as members of different social and cultural groups who contribute in numerous ways to the development of a society and its culture.

The theory's authors define dependency as a relationship in which the attainment of goals by one party is contingent on the resources of another party. People develop dependency relationships with the mass media as a way of attaining their goals of understanding, orientation, and play (Grant, Guthrie, & Ball-Rokeach, 1991). According to the theory, people develop expectations that the media can help them satisfy their needs. Thus, people develop "dependency relations" with the media (or a particular medium) that they believe will be most helpful in attaining a particular goal (Loges & Ball-Rokeach, 1993).

The theory identifies dependency relations on media information sources. Ball-Rokeach and DeFleur suggested that individuals depend on media for information in situations ranging from the need to identify the best buys at the supermarket to more general informational needs such as how to maintain a sense of "connection" with the world outside your neighborhood. The theory suggests that an individual's reliance on mass media develops when the person's informational needs on certain issues cannot be met by direct experience.

Media dependency is also linked to media *influence.* That is, the more important the media are to an individual, the more influence the media exert on that individual. Our society relies heavily on the mass media for information, entertainment, and the communication of societal norms and values. In our society, information is considered a prized commodity; we regard information as power. Today, most people use their personal computers to access information sources on the Internet. The theory recognizes, however, that dependency on the media varies greatly from one individual to another, from one group to another, and even from one culture to another.

A number of key assumptions about the media, the audience, and audience dependency have been identified: (a) if the media influence society it is because the media meet the audience's needs and wants, not because the media exert any "control" over individuals; (b) the uses people have for media in large part determine how much the media will influence them. For example, the more the audience depends on information from the media, the greater the likelihood the media will influence the audience's attitudes, beliefs, and even behavior; (c) because of the increasing complexity of modern society, we depend a great deal on the media to help us make sense of our world, to help us make decisions that allow us to cope better with life. The theory suggests further that we come to understand and even experience our world largely through the media. What a person learns about the world beyond their direct experience is influenced by the media. Our understanding of international politics, the global economy, and music, for example, are in part shaped by the content offered by the media (Baukus, 1996); (d) Individuals who have greater needs for information, escape, or fantasy will be more influenced by the media and have greater media dependency.

Ball-Rokeach and DeFleur suggested that media dependency ranges on a continuum from individuals who are totally dependent on the media to satisfy their needs to individuals who satisfy their needs independently from the media. (Remember that Shaw and McCombs addressed a similar concept with their *need for orientation.*) In addition, each individual displays variations within each category of media dependence. For example, you may depend heavily on news and newsmagazine shows for information yet have very little interest in escape and fantasy programs such as soap operas or situation comedies. Others may depend totally on the media for business news—monitoring sources such as CNN Business News, the Financial News Network, and CNBC, but ignoring the Weather Channel.

Most individuals are media dependent when conditions demand quick and accurate information. If you live in a climate that is prone to many tornadoes or hurricanes during the summer months or blizzards during the winter months, you may need an almost constant source of information about the weather. Your dependency on the media for weather-related information may even have stimulated you to purchase a "weather radio," which broadcasts bulletins and information from the local office of the National Weather Service. During times of weather-related crises, individuals become very dependent on the media.

Constant attention to and dependence on the media also emerged during the explosion of the space shuttle *Challenger* in 1986, the stock market crash of 1987, the war in the Persian Gulf in 1991, the bombing of the federal building in Oklahoma City in 1995, and the destruction of the World Trade Center by terrorists on September 11, 2001. Other crises, both local and national, also cause individuals to become more dependent on the media. For example, in the days following an airplane crash individuals tend to become more media dependent on the medium they believe will best satisfy their informational needs. For some this may mean purchasing national newspapers, such as *USA Today*, which will devote additional coverage to this type of story. For others, this may mean monitoring CNN throughout the day. Still others may turn to one of the many news-related websites to learn more details as they become available. Given the complex interactions of the individual, the media, and society, the social context often dictates the level of dependency. In times of conflict and uncertainty, the need for information increases, and dependency on the media also rises. During relatively calm periods of stability the audience relies less heavily on the media for guidance.

Media dependency is related to the complexity of the society in which a person lives. In a society as complex as ours, the media provide a number of essential functions: they provide information useful for the elections that are the centerpiece of democracy, they serve as whistle-blowers if the government oversteps its authority, they announce important economic or technological developments, they provide a window to the rest of the world, and they are a primary source of entertainment. The more functions served by the media, the more important they become.

Depending on the type of information goal a person has, he or she may choose one particular medium over another. Different media require different degrees of effort in satisfying one's informational goal. Preferences for particular media (for example, television, newspapers, Internet, or radio), differ according to information needs, the sources of media available, and the effort expended by the information seeker. For example, an individual may prefer to get information from television due to its immediacy, but because that medium may not be available in an office or an automobile, they must use radio instead. Some individuals choose newspapers over television because newspapers are perceived to cover stories in greater depth than television.

Media dependency theory asserts that the media have powerful effects on individuals and society. During the last decade several studies have investigated the assumptions of media dependency theory. One study investigated the union of media dependency theory and the theory of parasocial interaction discussed earlier. Grant, Guthrie, and Ball-Rokeach (1991) wondered if the development of parasocial interaction with a television personality increases the intensity of one's dependency on that medium or the reverse. Did an intense media dependency relationship stimulate the development of a parasocial interaction? They used the medium of television shopping (such as QVC and the Home Shopping Network) to investigate this relationship. One of the most important findings was that individuals who developed strong media dependency relationships with television shopping tended to develop parasocial relationships with television shopping personalities. In addition, they found that purchasing a product from a television shopping channel reinforced media dependency on that channel because it gave viewers a greater sense of connection to the show. The researchers also suggested that people tune in to television shopping not only to purchase products but to satisfy their entertainment goals and to learn about new products. The more the viewers had these goals, the more they watched, and the more parasocial interactions they developed with television shopping hosts.

Alan Rubin and Sven Windahl (1986) proposed a combination of uses and gratifications theory. They offered a "uses and dependency model," which incorporates elements of both theories. The uses and dependency model recognizes that the audience is somewhat active in their media-related behavior, and that individuals seek media that will fulfill personal needs. The model also represents the society-media-audience interaction and the mutual influences working to create interests and to influence the selection of particular media to satisfy goals. Needs are not always the sole product of the social and psychological characteristics of individuals; they are influenced by culture and society. This union of two theories also bridges the gap between the limited effects model of uses and gratifications and the powerful effects posited by dependency theory.

One test of the uses and dependency model found that "television dependents" contrasted with "newspaper dependents" (Baukus, 1996). Television dependents tend to see media coverage of conflict as "entertainment." This may account for why heavy television users may have been more likely to watch a great deal of coverage of the trial of O.J. Simpson or watch cable channels such as truTV. The study also found that television dependents believed the media are a source of information that helps us better understand the impact of social conflict on a community, country, or culture. Highly involved television-dependent groups differed from the other groups in their information belief. People who are highly involved *and* television dependent seem to want information as quickly as possible, and the ability of television to cover an event instantly with accompanying video is very important to this type of individual. Another study observed that dependency needs for understanding oneself and society were related to newspaper readership. Individuals who had greater need for understanding how society and its institutions function were more dependent on the newspaper than those without that need (Loges & Ball-Rokeach, 1993). Thus, media dependency theory helps us understand the relationships between the media and society, dependency relations with particular media, and the choice of particular media to satisfy information goals.

Media scholars have challenged media dependency theory on the grounds that it has "not yet been conclusively demonstrated that the experience of media dependency by average people is strongly related to a broad range of effects. Is there some ideal level of media dependency? Will new media increase our dependency or make us more independent?" (Baran & Davis, 1995, p. 229).

Theories of Mediated Interpersonal Communication

The impact of mediated communication on interpersonal communication is more dramatic today than ever before. The computer has emerged as the primary medium in which individuals interact with each other for both personal and professional communication. According to the Pew Internet and American Life report (Fallows, 2004) about 30 billion e-mails are sent every day, and 93% of Americans adult Internet users report using e-mail. This statistic supports the notion that much "interpersonal communication" is being conducted via that medium. One indication of this is that the number of phone messages professors receive from students has decreased dramatically, whereas the number of e-mail messages they receive has increased dramatically.

We are confident that many readers of this text have their own pages on "social networking" sites such as MySpace and Facebook, suggesting that people are using computer-mediated communication to fulfill social and interpersonal needs. Stefanone and Jang (2007) reported that even blogs are being widely adopted by individuals to engage in a form of mediated interpersonal communication.

The communication discipline has developed a number of scholars who identify their specialty as "CMC, or computer-mediated communication." The *Journal of Computer-Mediated Communication* (JCMC) is a Web-based, peer-reviewed scholarly journal whose focus is on social science research on computer-mediated communication via the Internet, the World Wide Web, and wireless technologies.

A Theory of Mediated Interpersonal Communication

The union of mass, or mediated, and interpersonal communication is not a new phenomena. As noted in the two-step flow theory, the individual plays a significant role in the mass communication process. Almost a quarter century ago, Gumpert and Cathcart (1986) examined the social and personal uses people have for mass communication. With the diffusion of computer-mediated communication, their theory is even more relevant today. Cathcart and Gumpert (1983) argued that media is not synonymous with mass communication (meaning communication over time and space to large numbers of people). They argued that the term *media* should not be excluded from other forms of human communication such as intrapersonal, interpersonal, group, or public. When we talk or text-message a friend or family member on the cell phone, we are using a medium to make our interaction possible. When using instant messaging or participating in an Internet chat group, we are engaged in mediated interpersonal and small-group communication.

Cathcart and Gumpert claimed (a) some interpersonal communication situations require media, (b) the media influence attitudes and behavior, (c) media content both reflects interpersonal behaviors and contains projections of them, and (d) the development of an individual's self-concept depends on the media. They offer the term "mediated interpersonal communication" to refer to any situation in which a mediated technology is used to replace face-to-face interaction. Cell phone conversations, text messaging, e-mail, the use of videoclips on YouTube, and even T-shirts are "media" that are used to facilitate interpersonal interaction. Another form of communication that bridges mediated and interpersonal forms are the teleparticipatory media, such as the terrestrial and satellite forms of two-way talk radio in which callers and the host(s) communicate with each other on the radio.

Gumpert and Cathcart's theory of mediated interpersonal communication emphasizes the pervasiveness of media and its importance as an element in interpersonal communication. It is gratifying to note that their call to theorists to incorporate the notion of media in their efforts to build theories of interpersonal and group communication has been heeded. One such theory, Social Information Processing Theory, is presented next.

Social Information Processing Theory

Social information processing theory (SIPT) represents a more contemporary theory that also addresses this phenomenon of mediated interpersonal communication. SIPT "explains how people get to know one another online, without nonverbal cues, and how they develop and manage relationships in the computer-mediated environment" (Walther, 2008, p. 391). The computer-mediated environment lacks the traditional nonverbal information that is exchanged in face-to-face (FTF) interaction. This nonverbal exchange provides invaluable sense-making feedback for the participants. In its absence, people interacting in the computer-mediated environment tend to group others as being either part of their in-group (i.e., people who share similar demographics, values, interests) or their out-group (i.e., people who do not share similar demographics, values, interests) (Reicher, Spears, & Postmes, 1995). According to Walther, SIPT predicts that "people may indeed get to know one another online, albeit more slowly and through different mechanisms than face to face interaction" (p. 392).

SIPT is based on two principle arguments. The first concerns impression-bearing (i.e., there is something in the information [misspellings, word choices, etc.] that makes an impression on the receiver) and the emotional, and relational management of information (Walther, 2003). In other words, we generally gather relational information, as opposed to task information, through non-verbal cues. When online, the nonverbal aspects are absent, so we must seek other ways of gathering such relational information. Therefore, it is also important to understand how nonverbal cues are translated into verbal and textual information. The second argument of SIPT reflects the rate of information that flows through computer-mediated communication (CMC) as compared to face-to-face communication. The main assumption about the rate of information is that when enough time has passed, and there are many communication exchanges between people, personal and relational information builds up and eventually renders CMC as equal to face-to-face communication in relational development and relational maintenance. For example, it is common for people to join computer dating services and make initial contact via computer-mediated communication. Consider Web sites such as Eharmony.com and Match.com, which serve as testaments to the effectiveness of romantic relationship development via CMC.

Another unique feature of SIPT concerns "the functions of impression-bearing and relational cues, and the degree to which nonverbal and verbal or textual cues may perform them" (Walther, 2008, p. 393). Previous theories of computer-mediated communication assume that due to the absence of nonverbal cues, people lose relational interest in each other as real people as well as lose the ability to relay information regarding descriptive, emotional, and personal information. Instead, SIPT assumes that people have an innate need to form impressions of other people, regardless of the medium being used. With nonverbal cues unavailable, people use surrogate communication systems to the point where the written word (via e-mail or text messaging) is considered the same as nonverbal cues. According to Walther (2008), SIPT considers time and rate differently from other theories of computer mediated communication in that "SIPT recognizes that verbal and textual cues are those that convey social and affective information in CMC, and that these written cues are the only cues to convey that information within text-based online communication" (p. 395). Unlike in face-to-face communication where there is a simultaneous exchange of verbal and nonverbal information (which can serve to accentuate, duplicate, or compliment messages), when verbal and nonverbal are restricted to one code as it is in CMC, the one code becomes responsible for the functions of other meaning transmission systems (e.g., occulesics [eye behavior], haptics, proxemics). As such, SIPT assumes that the rate of both social and task information are slower than FTF because people transmit less information per exchange. Thus, it takes more exchanges in computer-mediated communication to reach the same level of relational development that it does for FTF. Walther (1993) believes that this information exchange process is further hampered by the level of typing skills people possess as well as whether or not the mediated communication is synchronous (i.e., real-time exchange such as chat rooms and instant messaging) or asynchronous (i.e., time-delayed exchange such as e-mail).

SIPT treats communication symbols as interchangeable. In other words, besides nonverbal information, there are many other ways to express attitudes and emotions. As human beings are resourceful creatures, and in light of the absence of nonverbal information, people interacting via CMC cleverly utilize word content, word style, and message length, among other devices to fill the nonverbal void. This is not to suggest that CMC is deficient in the transfer of meaning as much as it takes more time to achieve the same goal when compared to the more rapid transfer of information that occurs during the multichanneled face-to-face communication.

The SIPT takes a developmental perspective on relationship development. That is, relationships develop as a process based on time and move from relational infancy to relational maturity. Given one of the main assumptions (i.e., a longer rate and time associated with the exchange of information in CMC compared to FTF), Walther (2008) made the logical connection that close relationships via CMC are going to take longer to develop than those of FTF. Walther argued that SIPT has a broad scope and is applicable to a host of CMC settings that include, among others, virtual work groups (Walther & Bunz, 2005), chat rooms (Henderson & Gilding, 2004), and online dating (Gibbs, Ellison, & Heino, 2006). Walther (2008) argued that "SIPT appears to be a popular theory of CMC for two contrasting reasons: (a) its intuitive application, on the one hand, and (b) its formal articulation of assumptions and propositions, on the other" (p. 399).

The future of SIPT, in terms of it refinement and extension, is based on technological advancement. For example, synchronous Webcams allow people to utilize nonverbal channels in real time. Thus, the future of SIPT is only constrained by what future technological developments may evolve. Another phenomenon is the popularity of social networking sites such as Facebook and MySpace. According to Walther (2008), these forums hold unique challenges for SIPT regarding whether or not the theoretical assumptions of the theory hold true in these CMC venues. Interpersonal factors such as interpersonal deception is also a potential fruitful avenue for the test of social information processing theory. According to deception scholars such as Buller and Burgoon (1996, interpersonal deception theory) and Ekman (1985, leakage hypothesis), much of deception takes place via nonverbal channels. Given that SIPT compensates for nonverbal communicating through other avenues, investigating deception over a variety of CMC venues should prove fruitful in the extension and further development of social information processing theory.

References

Ball-Rokeach, S. J.. & DeFleur, M. L. (1976). A dependency model of mass-media effects. *Communication Research, 3*, 3–21.

Ball-Rokeach, S. J., Power. G. J., Guthrie. K. K., & Waring, H. R. (1990). Value-framing abortion in the United States: An application of media system dependency theory. *International Journal of Public Opinion Research, 2*, 249–273.

Baran, S. J., & Davis, D. K. (1995). *Mass communication theory.* Belmont. CA: Wadsworth Publishing Company.

Baukus, R. A. (1996). *Perception of mediated social conflict: Media dependency and involvement.* Unpublished manuscript, the Pennsylvania State University.

Blumler, J. G. (1979). The role of theory in uses and gratifications studies. *Communication Research, 6*, 9–36.

Cathcart, R., & Gumpert, G. (1983). Mediated interpersonal communication: Toward a new typology. *Quarterly Journal of Speech, 69*, 267–277.

Cohen, B. (1963). *The press and foreign policy.* Princeton: Princeton University Press.

DeFleur, M. L., & Ball-Rokeach, S. (1982). *Theories of mass communication* (4th ed.). New York: Longman.

Donohew, L., Palmgreen, P., & Rayburn, J. D. (1987). Social and psychological origins of media use: A lifestyle analysis. *Journal of Broadcasting and Electronic Media, 31*, 255–278.

Flew, T. (2002). *Newmedia.* Melbourne, Australia: Oxford University Press.

Gerbner, G., & Gross, L. (1976a). Living with television: The violence profile. *Journal of Communication, 26*, 172–199.

Gerbner, G., & Gross, L. (1976b). The scary world of TV's heavy viewer. *Psychology Today*, pp. 41–45, 89.

Gerbner, G., Gross, L., Morgan, M., & Signorielli, N. (1980). The "mainstreaming" of America: Violence profile no. 11. *Journal of Communication, 30*, 10–29.

Gerbner, G., Gross, L., Morgan, M., & Signorielli, N. (1986). Living with television: The dynamics of the cultivation process. In J. Bryant & D. Zillmann (Eds.). *Perspectives on media effects* (pp. 17–40). Hillsdale, NJ: Lawrence Erlbaum.

Glynn, C. J., & McLeod, J. M. (1985). Implications of the spiral of silence theory for communication and public opinion research. In K. R. Sanders, L. L. Kaid, & D. Nimmo (Eds.), *Political communication yearbook 1984* (pp. 43–65). Carbondale, IL: Southern Illinois University Press.

Glynn, C. J., Hayes, A. F., & Shanahan, J. (1997). Perceived support for one's opinions and willingness to speak out: A meta-analysis of survey studies on the "spiral of silence." *Public* Opinion *Quarterly, 61*, 452–463.

Gonzenbach, W. J., King, C., & Jablonski. P. (1999). Homosexuals and the military: An analysis of the spiral of silence. *The Howard Journal of Communications, 10*, 281–296.

Grant, A. E., Guthrie. K. K., & Ball-Rokeach, S. J. (1991). Television shopping: A media system dependency perspective. *Communication Research, 18*, 773–798.

Hawkins, R. P., & Pingree, S. (1982). Television's influence on social reality. In D. Pearl, L. Bouthilet, & J. Lazar (Eds.), *Television and behavior: Ten years of scientific progress and implications for the eighties: Vol. 2. Technical reviews* (pp. 224–247). Washington. DC: U.S. Government Printing Office.

Horton, D., & Wohl, R. R. (1956). Mass communication and parasocial interaction: Observations on intimacy at a distance. *Psychiatry, 19*, 215–229.

Hughes, M. (1980). The fruits of cultivation analysis: A reexamination of some effects of television watching. *Public Opinion Quarterly, 44*, 287–302.

Jeffres, L. W., Neuendorf, K. A., & Atkin, D. (1999). Spirals of silence: Expressing opinions when the climate of opinion is unambiguous. *Political Communication, 16*, 115–131.

Johnston, J., & Ettema, J. S. (1986). Using television to best advantage: Research for prosocial television. In J. Bryant & D. Zillmann (Eds.), *Perspectives on media effects* (pp. 143–164). Hillsdale, NJ: Lawrence Erlbaum.

Katz, E., & Lazarsfeld, P. F. (1955). *Personal influence: The part played by people in the flow of mass communication.* New York: Free Press.

Lasswell, H. D. (1927). *Propaganda technique in world wars.* New York: Knopf.

Lasswell, H. D. (1948). The structure and function of communication in society. In L. Bryson (Ed.), *The communication of ideas* (pp. 37–51). New York: Harper.

Lazarsfeld, P. F. & Stanton, F. N. (1944). *Radio research 1942–1943.* New York: Duel, Sloan, and Pearce.

Lazarsfeld, P. F., Berelson, B. R., & Gaudet, H. (1944). *The people's choice: How the voter makes up his mind in a presidential campaign.* New York: Columbia University Press.

Levy, M. R. (1979). Watching TV news as parasocial interaction. *Journal of Broadcasting, 23,* 69–80.

Lin, C. A., & Salwen, M. B. (1997). Predicting the spiral of silence on a controversial public issue. *The Howard Journal of Communications, 8,* 129–141.

Lippman, W. (1922). *Public opinion.* New York: Macmillan.

Loevinger, L. (1979). The ambiguous mirror: The reflective-projective theory of broadcasting and mass communication. In G. Gumpert & R. Cathcart (Eds.), *Inter/Media: Interpersonal communication in a media world* (pp. 234–260). New York: Oxford University Press.

Loges, W. E., & Ball-Rokeach, S. J. (1993). Dependency relations and newspaper readership. *Journalism Quarterly, 70,* 602–614.

Lowery, S., & DeFleur, M. L. (1995). *Milestones in mass communication research: Media effects* (3rd ed.). New York: Longman.

McCombs, M. E., & Shaw, D. L. (1972). The agenda-setting function of mass media. *Public Opinion Quarterly, 36,* 176–187.

McDonald, D. G., Glynn, C. J., Kim, S., & Ostman, R. E. (2001). The spiral of silence in the 1948 Presidential election. *Communication Research, 28,* 139–155.

McQuail, D. (1984). With the benefit of hindsight: Reflections on uses and gratifications research. *Critical Studies in Mass Communication, 1,* 177–193.

Noelle-Neumann, E. (1984). *The spiral of silence: Public opinion—Our social skin.* Chicago, IL: University of Chicago Press.

Noll, A. M. (2007). *The evolution of media.* Lanham, MD: Rowman & Littlefield.

Perse, E. M. (2001). *Media effects and society.* Mahwah, NJ: L. Erlbaum.

Perse, E. M., & Rubin, R. B. (1989). Attribution in social and parasocial relationships. *Communication Research, 16,* 59–77.

Potter, W. J. (1986). Perceived reality and the cultivation hypothesis. *Journal of Broadcasting and Electronic Media, 30,* 159–174.

Reicher, S., Spears, R., & Postmes, T. (1995). A social identity model of deindividuation phenomena. *European Review of Social Psychology, 6,* 161–198.

Rogers, E. M. (1995). *Diffusion of innovations* (4th ed.). New York: Free Press.

Rubin, A. M. (1979). Television use by children and adolescents. *Human Communication Research, 5,* 109–120.

Rubin, A. M. (1983). Television uses and gratifications: The interactions of viewing patterns and motivations. *Journal of Broadcasting, 27,* 37–51.

Rubin, A. M. (1984). Ritualized and instrumental television viewing. *Journal of Communication, 34,* 67–77.

Rubin, A. M., Perse, E. M., & Powell, R. A. (1985). Loneliness, parasocial interaction, and local television news viewing. *Human Communication Research, 12,* 155–180.

Rubin, A. M., & Rubin, R. B. (1985). Interface of personal and mediated communication: A research agenda. *Critical Studies in Mass Communication, 2,* 36–53.

Rubin, A. M., & Windahl, S. (1986). The uses and dependency model of mass communication. *Critical Studies in Mass Communication, 3,* 184–199.

Rubin, R. B., & McHugh, M. P. (1987). Development of parasocial interaction relationships. *Journal of Broadcasting and Electronic Media, 31,* 279–292.

Salmon, C. T., & Glynn, C. J. (1996). Spiral of silence: Communication and public opinion as social control. In M. B. Salwen & D. W. Stacks (Eds.), *An integrated approach to communication theory and research* (pp. 165–180). Mahwah. NJ: L. Erlbaum.

Salmon, C. T., & Moh, C. Y. (1992). The spiral of silence: Linking individual and society through communication. In J. D. Kennamer (Ed.), *Public opinion, the press, and public policy* (pp. 145–161). Westport, CT: Praeger.

Scheufele, D. A., & Moy, P. (2000). Twenty-five years of the spiral of silence: A conceptual review and empirical outlook. *International Journal of Public Opinion Research, 12,* 3–28.

Schramm, W. (Ed.). (1954). *The process and effects of mass communication.* Urbana: University of Illinois Press.

Schramm, W., Lyle, J.. & Parker. E. (1961). *Television in the lives of our children.* Palo Alto, CA: Stanford University Press.

Severin, W. J., & Tankard, J. W. (2001). *Communication theories: Origins, methods and uses in the mass media* (5th ed.). Boston: Allyn & Bacon.

Shaw, D. L., & McCombs, M. E. (1977). The emergence of American political issues: The agenda-setting function of the press. St. Paul, MN: West Publishing Co.

Turner, J. R. (1993). Interpersonal and psychological predictors of parasocial interaction with different television performers. *Communication Quarterly, 41,* 443–453.

Walther, J. B. (2008). Social information processing theory: Impressions and relationship development online. In L. A. Baxter & D. O. Braithwaite (Eds.), *Engaging theories in interpersonal communication: Multiple perspectives* (pp. 391–404). Thousand Oaks, CA: Sage.

Walther, J. B., & Bunz, U. (2005). The rules of virtual groups: Trust, liking, and performance in computer-mediated communication. *Journal of Communication, 55,* 828–846.

Weaver, D. (1987). Media agenda-setting and elections: Assumptions and implications. In D. L. Paletz (Ed.), *Political communication research* (pp. 176–193). Norwood, NJ: Ablex.

Weaver, D. H., Graber, D. A., McCombs, M. E.. & Eyal, C. H. (1981). *Media agenda setting in a presidential election: Issues, images, and interest.* New York: Praeger.

Windahl, S. (1981). Uses and gratifications at the crossroads. In G. C. Wilhoit & H. deBock (Eds.), *Mass Communication Review Yearbook* (Vol. 2, pp. 174–185). Beverly Hills: Sage.

Wright, C. R. (1960). Functional analysis and mass communication. *Public Opinion Quarterly, 24,* 606–620.

CHAPTER 4

Social Media: Living in the Revolution

> The people we attempted to reach over the years appear before our eyes as if they are long-lost friends and relatives. The faceless have revealed their identities through their actions and words.
>
> —*Brian Solis, Engage*

Social media dramatically changed advertising, public relations, branding, and marketing communication models. Again, the entire dynamic has flipped. Today the consumer is more in charge of marketing messages. It's no longer business as usual. If they expect to compete for market share and mind share in the future, marketing executives and entrepreneurs must continue to experiment with finding new ways to integrate social media into their marketing mix.

Social media have leveled the playing field. Their effect has not only changed marketing, they have shaken up everything, particularly media and media business models. Sociologists and anthropologists suggest we're in the midst of a social revolution (Hansen & Shneiderman, 2011). Arab Spring and Occupy Wall Street are two good examples that will be discussed later in the chapter. The wake-up call has been delivered.

The Reach of Social Media

No matter all the applications and social media options, the fact is that content is what drives and propagates messages. For starters, let's look at three examples of some remarkable content. The first two are pro bono pieces that do a remarkable job of visual storytelling. They're personal, meaningful, honest, and compelling. Their form and content are equally powerful. Both of them address the problem of potable water; although the messages are the same, the graphic solutions are as creative and memorable as they are different.

Solidarites International is a humanitarian organization that provides aid and assistance to victims of war or natural disaster. The association has concentrated its action on meeting three vital needs:

https://www.youtube
.com/watch?v=h35Gb1
MWqdY&list=UUugRv
yawnOI9eL6vU0PrxNA.

water, food, and shelter. The content of the following URL on the dangers of unsafe drinking water is compelling. Not only is it the kind of content many would be inclined to share with others, the online videos offer optional links to export to Twitter and Facebook.

The second video provides equally valuable information quickly and memorably. Like most good stories, it has a compelling beginning, an engaging story, and a surprising end. Are you converted? Would you pass on these very important social messages on your social media channels to friends?

The third online video, "A Drama Surprise on a Quiet Square," was produced in a little town in Belgium on a square where nothing really happens. They placed a button, "Push to add drama," that creates a story full of surprises. It is beautifully directed and filmed. It's an exemplary viral marketing clip that not only communicates "get your drama at TNT" but breaks down television genres. The consumer is a big part of the production, driving it in the viral video—and literally by passing it around on social media.

https://www
.youtube.com/
watch?v=
77Mv8pauMKc

The Perfect Storm: Where Did Social Media Come From?

The seeds of social media were planted deeply years ago via the inventions of transistors, computer chips, microprocessors, and the Internet. The long-established hierarchy between the consumer and media and marketing began to shift—gradually but imminently.

Consider the magnitude of this transformation. Over the course of roughly 60 years, computers have advanced from Atanasoff's 700-pound computer (Narins, 2001) to today's compact and portable laptops, iPads, and electronic hand-held devices. Since then, scientists, media professionals, and inventors developed countless breakthroughs in computer language, storage, mainframe computers, software, networking, robots, artificial intelligence, and microprocessors. That is only a short list of areas where substantial changes were realized.

In the 1980s, the use of personal computers and their sales rocketed. In 1982, *Time* magazine broke its traditional "Man of the Year" cover and instead celebrated the personal computer with a "Machine of the Year" issue. Audiences began changing their patterns of media usage, increasingly gravitating toward the Internet and its growing options not available in other media. What's more, it was generally free.

https://www
.youtube.com/
watch?v=316AzLYfAzw

What happened was a slow but sure growth of personal computers and—starting with email—social media. Concurrently, the traditional media were experiencing a slow meltdown as its audiences continued to fragment. Newspapers tried everything to recoup the loss in ad revenue and sales: new, faster presses; small formats; and finally creating their own websites. Sales and circulation continued to plummet. Many newspapers had a choice between continuing to lose capital, go out of business, or be put up for sale.

Media companies began to buy and sell each other, and over time some companies acquired or built a chain of newspapers, broadcast outlets, and other media. Media conglomerates added businesses unrelated to media to their holdings. But often conglomerates struggled to make their media properties profitable. Consequently, media began changing hands again when they struggled financially—which was one of the reasons GE sold its media companies to Comcast in 2010.

Parallel to the audience migration and growth of computer usage, media convergence was blooming. By 1980, the industries of print and publishing, computers and broadcasting and motion pictures began to converge (Aspray, 1997). The newspapers' remaining audiences were aging and literally dying, and newspapers continued to struggle financially. Many magazines suffered similarly, and they continued to invent new niche audiences. With print readership and circulation declining and TV's market share ratings falling, and audiences fragmenting, advertising dollars disappeared. Media companies began to buy and sell each other. Over those same years, digital technology exploded. Twenty years later, all three areas have merged; film, print, and broadcast products are accessible through the Internet on a laptop computer, electronic tablet, and a smartphone.

Much of mainstream media and business didn't see this convergent storm of change on their radar. The short version is that the old business model for media, marketing, and advertising has changed, and in the process, the power shifted from publishers to consumers.

Shadow of Liberty

http://shadowsofliberty.org/watch/

> "Focus on how to be social, not on how to do social."
> Convince & Convert—*Jay Baer*

Keep It Personal

Social media have changed marketing. The many-to-one marketing communication paradigm is gone. It's a flip from mass communication to two-way conversations. Advertising and marketing is longer a monologue; instead, it is a dialogue in which marketers no longer control their corporate message (Safko, 2012). That's a message some marketing and advertising agencies haven't heeded—yet.

The old manifesto of marketing meant advertising. Public relations people tried to get print or broadcast media to use handouts. For the most part, mediated marketing meant the same old one-way ad-speak that relied on poking them, interrupting them to get their attention. Sure, it mixed it up by different advertising campaigns selling their products, but despite all the noise, clever pitches, bright four-color, million-dollar TV productions and ad campaigns, the marketing messages were invisible. The louder and more constant the advertising became, the less people listened. Research and carefully weighed psychographics and demographics still pigeonholed consumers. They are the "long-lost" faceless folks Brian Solis refers to in his quotation at the beginning of this chapter.

Consumers didn't really watch, read, listen to, or process conventional marketing messages. They screened the telemarketing calls at dinner with their answering machines. What do you do with the direct mail you receive? It isn't called "junk mail" for nothing. Email marketing is largely blocked with spam filters, and typically what might get through is color-coded and ends up going where the direct mail went. Trapped in the private space of their cars, consumers dodge the unwanted radio commercials by muting or turning down the volume. At home, their NFL game, soaps, and movies are interrupted by TV commercials. The ads mean bathroom break time—or another trip to the refrigerator.

Recently, I purchased a new car. I'd seen one on the street and liked its sleek styling, so I opened my online *Consumer Reports* account to see how they compared to other sedans in their class. They gave it a "best buy." But I wanted more information, so I visited the Edmunds Forums site. It's free, thorough, offers user groups (based on the model, make, and year of the car) and related links. Then I sought out other owners and read about their experiences and opinions of the automobile. I scrolled and clicked through them long enough to be convinced it was a fine car. Ultimately, I drove to the dealership for a test drive and made an offer and returned home. Two days later, the salesman phoned to say the sales manager had accepted my offer. My car purchasing experience was nothing like previous ones, thankfully.

That doesn't mean I avoided glossy magazine ads and occasional TV spots for this car. If nothing else, they reinforced my decision to buy. It also doesn't mean that traditional advertising should be arbitrarily discarded. It can still work. And who knows? Perhaps another advertising Renaissance will suddenly bloom—one similar (in effect, anyway) to the creative revolution of the 1950s and '60s.

Ad agencies the likes Wieden + Kennedy, BBH, and Crispin Porter Bogusky are trying to push the envelope, to make ads relevant, believable, and engaging. It should also be pointed out that those same agencies have embraced social media and experimenting with new and exciting ways to use it. Nonetheless, ad avoidance is increasing. The general reaction to direct mail, radio, and print ads discussed earlier certainly supports the increasing swell of backlash (Anderson, 2010). Technologies the likes of DVRs, Tivo, and programmed taping will increase.

Social media have changed the way consumers make their decisions. A component of social media is social networking. Here communities of people hang out with friends on Twitter, MySpace, Facebook, and Linked-In. These days, instead of getting product information from mediated marketing, they're embracing and trusting social media. They've been skeptical of advertising, anyway. Where do they get product information? Users want to know what their friends, colleagues, and online community find relevant about a product. Social networking is a quick and easy avenue to amass important information, and consumers readily share information with each other. It saves time and energy, minimizes frustration, and the information received through social networking is more trusted.

Advertising agency Bartle Bogle Hegarty (BBH, New York) used social media to propel an integrated, media-rich campaign for the launch of Oasis' seventh album "Dig Out Your Soul."

Kevin Roddy and Calle and Pelle Sjonell worked as creative directors (CDs) for the "Dig Out Your Soul" project; all three were CDs at BBH. Pelle Sjonell talked about where they drew from and what shaped their creative strategy. Pelle explained their rationale and "what ifs?":

Calle and I sat down and thought the music industry needed help since many had stopped inventing how to market their releases after the advent of iTunes. We were inspired by Radiohead who had released their album and having people buy it at the price they thought it was worth—genius. But that was more of a comment to the times than about the music itself. So we thought, If a song is super successful, it will travel through all the filters of fame in music. It will be a highly played single on radio, being a "high rotation" music video; and if you're really lucky, someone might pick it as their karaoke song. Eventually, the biggest form of success is if someone will actually play your song making a living on the streets as a street performer. So we thought, *What if we start there?*

In effect, they were doing a "reverse launch," and they would take the music and the entire project to the streets of New York City. Kevin Roddy explains: "This is a great example of new thinking applied to an album launch, a sort of backwards album release—where the music starts on the streets instead of ending up there."

But there was more: In addition, the BBH team would document the entire experience—from selecting street musicians, to interviews with members of Oasis, live street performances, fan interaction, and the street music itself to tell the story of the entire production.

The concept was to find talented buskers (street musicians) and have members of Oasis teach them the songs from the new album and have them debut the songs at strategic subway stations, including Penn Station, Astor Place, Grand Central Station, and (of course) Times Square. It was the perfect venue for a lot of reasons, including the fact that New York City is the capital of street culture.

The result was "Dig out Your Soul in the Streets," the HD documentary launched on MySpace. The BBH team—along with documentary filmmakers, Emmett and Brendan Malloy (HSI Productions), director of photography Sam Levy, and film editor Tim Wheeler (Three Foot Giant)—collaborated to produce the film. You can see the entire documentary film on YouTube.

By good fortune and pure coincidence, BBH was involved with producing a separate advertising campaign promoting New York City. (Mark Svartz details that separate work—"C'mon, LeBron!"—at the end of the chapter. It also happens to embrace social media in some inventive ways.)

Dig out Your Soul in the Streets

https://www.youtube
.com/watch?v=
CC5HI6D53XU

Pelle Sjonell continues:

We were creative directors for the New York City project at the time as well . . . the official unit responsible for tourism advertising under City Hall and Mayor Bloomberg. They had an open brief to us that if we could prove that New York is the most vibrant interesting city in the world, we'd tell them how—but it couldn't be an ad. We'd have to *prove* it. Great we thought: This would be perfect for the city but we need a band and an album. So we contacted Brad Gelforn who was responsible for marketing at Warner Brothers Music. He was also a friend of BBH. Then he landed Oasis and off we went. So there were *two* clients.

Next, members of Oasis were flown to NYC. They listened to the street buskers and coached the acts in the morning and then they'd spread out across the city to perform. The city received free publicity, a big bump in traffic, and the album became the first U.S. top-10 album for Oasis in 10 years.

Social media were key. The team completely believed in their idea, the client, and music—and mostly, they trusted the consumers who would largely produce and distribute the advertising campaign via social media. Information about Oasis and street musician performances were loaded on to Oasis fan websites. Then New York City Tourism's site nycgo.com offered fans a page where they could use Google Maps and Google Earth to find the live performances. Fans were encouraged to upload their own videos of the performances to a dedicated YouTube channel. They made the videos and shared them with fans and others on MySpace.

It was an interesting chemistry: rock and roll, street culture, buskers, and social media all mixed together. The band's seventh album, *Dig out Your Soul*, was launched in 2008 through live performances on the streets of New York, news on Oasis fan sites, and a documentary distributed globally on MySpace.

> "You are what you tweet."
>
> Monkey Inferno—*Alex Tew*

Social Media Have Few Rules

Over the years, some of that "free spirit" in social media ran into legal problems. The court ordered Napster (a file-sharing peer-to-peer service for downloading music encoded in MP-3 formats) to shut down over copyright infringement rights. During its existence (1999–2001), it was one of the busiest services on the Internet. In fact, it was so popular on college campuses that systems administrators blocked access to Napster to relieve bandwidth congestion. It was an overnight phenomenon and caused a great deal of social and legal controversy.

YouTube initiated "an online video revolution" beginning in 2006. That same year marked the introduction of both Facebook and Twitter. Apple launched its iPhone in 2007 and the iPad in 2010. A short list of some of the more widely used social networks includes Facebook, Flickr, Fotolog, FourSquare, Google+, LivingSocial, MySpace, StumbleUpon, Twitter, Tumblr, and Yahoo!Pulse.

The Internet has socialized communication. That's one of the benefits and unique properties of social media: ownership. And not just ownership in the sense that the Internet is free and every user has a stake in it, but in that social networks empower everyone. It provides the average person a voice, one that can be widely shared, even on a global scale. The Internet has no boundaries. Indeed, it was initially dedicated to promoting and maintaining a free and open Web—one without outside governance.

The Social Revolution

However, social media are much more than the stereotype many people have of it: anelectronic café where people chat at their leisure, text, play video or virtual reality games, and share photos on a grand scale. Those activities are common to social media; however, its design and fabric is based on sharing: community, communication, collaboration, and freedom.

But the possibilities of this new Global Village are virtually endless. The Internet and social media helped spark revolutions in marketing, politics, business, journalism, and many other areas. The Web disseminates information with lightning speed—everywhere—which helps shape a new social and political dynamic. Now government has a difficult time keeping information from its citizens.

Social media and the Internet confirm the notion that we no longer need to seek out news; it will find us. The first photo of US Airways' crash into the Hudson River in January of 2009 was shot with an iPhone and uploaded on Twitter's Twitpic by Janis Krums. He was aboard a ferry, visiting New York City (http://latimesblogs.latimes.com/technology/2009/01/citizen-photo-o.html). Today, disasters, tragedies, revolution, and other cutting-edge news is reaching the mainstream public faster than traditional modern media can publish or broadcast it.

In early 2011, social media would fuel the Arab Spring. Discontent had been building across the Middle East. The event that ignited protests across the Arab world—from Tunisia to Egypt to Algeria—began with a Tunisian man setting himself on fire after the police publically humiliated him and shut down his alleged illegal fruit stand. That 27-year-old vendor is now a national and regional hero. Mohammed Bouazizi's act of desperation incited demonstrations and riots throughout Tunisia in protest of longstanding social and political issues. Social media spread news of the incident, subsequent protests, and the ousting of then-President Zine El Abidine Ben Ali. The successful Tunisian protests led to additional self-immolations in several other Middle Eastern and North African countries.

Some of the strongest protests erupted in Egypt, where discontent had been smoldering for years. The uprising was largely a campaign of nonviolent pro-democracy demonstrations, marches, and strikes. In response, President Hosni Mubarak and the Egyptian government attempted to crush the protests through arrests, beatings, and clashes with the demonstrators. Then, in an attempt to cut off communication of the turmoil—information going out and coming into the country—Mubarak severed mobile and Web communications throughout the country, starting with Telecom Egypt. He didn't want social media via Facebook and Twitter to spread word of what was occurring in Cairo.

Wael Ghonim, Middle Eastern Google marketing and product manager, had seen enough. He'd been appalled by the system's history of corruption, the government's state-controlled media, and average citizens being tortured and murdered. Then a demonstrator, Khaled Said, was brutally murdered. After Said's death, Ghonim posted, "We Are All Khaled Said" on Facebook. It briefly chronicled his police abduction and posted a series of appalling photos and video, some of which had been shot with a cell phone in the morgue (BBC, 2011).

The post received more than a half-million hits. Other Egyptians took to Facebook, adding countless accounts of kidnappings, beatings, torture, and other travesties perpetrated on ordinary citizens. It became a flashpoint. Egyptians mobilized in unprecedented numbers.

The rest is history. Likewise, social media in Libya, Tunisia, Bahrain, Syria, and other Middle-Eastern countries rallied citizens to stand up for their human rights via social media. Mubarak was forced to step down, and eventually he was tried in court and imprisoned.

Later Ghonim spoke with CNN's Wolf Blitzer:

> I want to meet Mark Zuckerberg one day and thank him. . . . I'm talking on behalf of Egypt. This revolution started online. This revolution started on Facebook. This revolution started in June 2010 when hundreds of thousands of Egyptians started collaborating content. We would post a video on Facebook that would be shared by 60,000 people on their walls within a few hours. I've always said that if you want to liberate a society just give them the Internet. (Quoted in Cohen, 2011)

Like Bouazizi, Ghonim became a national hero and a symbol of the Egyptian movement.

Protestors at Home

Social media have been an important tool for protesters overseas. However, recently social media helped organize and mobilize thousands of people in New York City. Impassioned protesters used Facebook and Twitter to take their message and concerns to the street. The number of Occupy Wall Street demonstrators swelled as citizens from around the country headed to New York.

Ironically, however, it was mainstream media that latched on to the event and really brought it to the attention of Americans and international communities through traditional media channels. Interestingly enough, it was the content from Facebook and Twitter that drew in the national and international coverage of the protests in Manhattan. But at the heart of things, it was the social media dynamic that gave Occupy Wall Street the impetus to land on page one and run as the lead feature in broadcast coverage. The movement would gain national momentum. This wasn't just another protest story; it was another example of how social media are figuring into our social, political, economic, and cultural consciousness.

"People are listening," says Ronn Torossian, CEO of 5WPR, a New York PR agency. "When the president of the United States pays attention, this is no longer a fringe event. Digital chatter has reached a critical mass." Regardless of how you stand politically, you have to marvel at how "community" and social networking worked to accomplish what the protesters set out to do. It was unique, too, that the movement was leaderless, which speaks again to the sense of equality in social media communities and reflects dramatic changes in communication brought on by the social media revolution.

Using Social Media Creatively

Many other areas in communication are affected by the change as well. Marketing and advertising are still trying to figure out how to reach these communities using social media. So far they haven't cracked the case. To date, the vast majority of advertising you see on the Internet still uses the old rules of marketing. It looks and is still perceived as advertising. It is generally considered annoying. Most of the current Internet advertising is targeted at a mass audience, and it's still one-way and disruptive.

Oddly enough, marketers don't seem to understand or care that customers resent ads that interrupt them. The primary strategy employed for Web advertising employs banners, pop-ups, interstitial pages, and other ways to attract attention: bright colors, flashing background, rotating graphics, ambushes that slide out from the side, fading, and other ploys. **Interstitial ads** are full-page ads that suddenly appear out of nowhere between leaving one website and arriving at another. They disappear if not clicked on; sometimes they appear upon leaving a website. They're considered less obnoxious. Most detested are small ads that suddenly appear on your computer (usually in the middle of your screen) that have their close buttons hidden within the ad's design. They force you to stop your reading (or whatever it is you're doing) to search for the small exit (X) box. Another ploy is to flash a "Do you really want to leave this page?" message, with directions that seem counterintuitive, thus keeping you there longer. RIA (Rich Internet Applications) ads generally employ Adobe Flash for animation, video, interaction, or some combination thereof. Of all of these, they are the most expensive by far and often can be much more inviting and better designed than the banner ads. The latter are cheaper and much less sophisticated in terms of both their design and content. They also clutter most Web pages.

There is, however, some really engaging and creative advertising on the Internet. The most successful are personal, loaded with rich content, and interactive. Their flexibility and options are friendly. Many are useful to marketers and customers. Multimedia is often used. The work is well-conceived and multifaceted.

Perhaps one of the finest examples of Internet marketing is Starbuck's "My Starbucks Idea." Structurally, it is a blog, forum, and interactive site. Starbucks uses the Internet and social media to start (and maintain over time) a meaningful conversation with their customers.

My Starbucks Idea

http://mystarbucksidea
.force.com

The website allows people to gather unbiased information, explore, find, and obtain a wider range of Starbucks product. Additionally, it allows users an opportunity to create another community of interesting people. It seeks the opinions and ideas of those who visit their "Internet café," asking them to tell them what they want from Starbucks. "What can we do to make your experience better?" Members have a virtual suggestion box (MyStarbucks-Idea), and Starbucks encourages them to share their ideas, tell them what they think of other people's suggestions, and join a discussion. It's akin to getting coffee at one of their cafes. It's a hangout, an inviting, laid-back place with good music, free wifi, great pastries, and a "cool" forum to meet new people or meet up with friends. Like the cafes, it offers a wide variety of Starbucks merchandise, including music. At the site you can watch beautifully shot videos of performances and casual interviews with some of the artists whose music Starbucks has anthologized. Product is all over the place, but no one's pushing it at you. The site is as neat, organized, and relaxed as the cafes. Both reflect the brand. Speaking of which, Starbucks ranks sixth on the Top Ten Brands of Facebook members (Indvik, 2011).

My Starbucks Idea reflects the new marketing manifesto. They're thinking about how they can change or introduce things to make your next visit to Starbucks even better. We aren't being told how great their product is or being told about the benefits of their coffee. It's a conversation, and they are marketing more than coffee.

The Visual Tools of Social Media

> Video is the new frontier, and again, it's powered by the socialization of content. The ability to produce and publish online video is universal and the networks that host them can extend the reach of any person or brand globally, facilitating connections based on the content in a practically limitless array.
>
> Engage—*Brian Solis*

Video and other social media graphic formats provide an array of options for visual communication. For brevity purposes, let's examine three basic categories you can use. In fact, very few media formats cannot be integrated visually into the Internet and social media.

Social networks have numerous graphic capabilities and can use the tools listed in the following sections, so figure them among your visual options—if for nothing else as entrepreneurial delivery options, which are also efficient and well traveled.

Facebook, YouTube, Twitter, MySpace, and new offshoots contribute significantly to the visual side of social media. Photos are part of the nucleus of Facebook. Other social media use the same tactic. Their payoffs extend well beyond posting photographs, videos, and a lot of mundane content. Social media take on a multitude of forms: forums, blogs,podcasts, journals, visual imagery, wikis, email, wallpostings, vlogs, and more. While platforms and content vary, they tend to be graphic in nature and narrative based. The two primary workhorses, however, are photography and video.

Photography

Photographic imagery is everywhere, including in social media. It delivers as much satisfaction for us on the Internet as it does in our real lives. One of the first things we share with others is photography—family, friends, vacations, and images of one another. We are visually predisposed and curious by nature. Consequently, it's only natural that we want to see the persona behind the blog, SMS, or social network.

Photographs capture time; in that sense, they may be archival, whether through formal visual documentation or family scrapbooks. Photography opens a graphic door into our personal world. Flikr, PhotoSwarm, SmugMug, Photobucket, RedBucket, and Picasa are fine photo sites. That said, obviously, Facebook fits—in more of a social sense. If you're a photographer looking to share your portfolio or images, LinkedIn network would be an excellent consideration.

http://www
.maryellenmark.com/

Speaking of portfolios, if you want to see one the best organized, functional yet engaging photo websites, literally and figuratively, go to Mary Ellen Mark's site. It is as beautiful and intuitive as it is austere. Mark is perhaps the most celebrated woman photographer in the world and one of the most influential. Her work (largely black and white) straddles photographic genres: documentary, photojournalism, portraiture, advertising, and other commercial work.

Examine the site, but be prepared to spend some time there. The page format itself is wide, clean, and welcoming. It's framed with a generous white mat to set off and call your attention to the photo space in the center. Running across the top, in neat, legible sans serif type, are the content headings of the page: home, books, gallery, store, exhibitions, lectures, workshops, bio, and contact. All diminutive but easily found and read.

Each of her books opens up and allows you to examine the entirety of every photograph—page by page, including text. There are navigational arrows on the bottom right. Above the directional (top left) is a small green "share" button. Each of the photographs carries identification: title (along with a caption on some images), place, date, and file number. Galleries have prices beneath the hand-printed imagery and the store merchandise as well. Everything—including the cost of each item—is understated. Along with being an artist and documentarian, she is an excellent marketer. Mary Ellen Mark is also a brand. What brand characteristics come to mind?

Slideshows are another wonderful option with social media, and they can be presented in numerous ways. Another interesting approach is to incorporate sound—perhaps even layered with narrative and music. It doesn't have quite the power of video or film, but it's an interesting option in photo storytelling.

Perhaps moving pictures can tell much better stories, not only via motion picture and documentary films but through social media video. Sasquatch advertising integrated all of its Widmer "Open Source Brewing" launch using print, video, documentary, recipes, *and* social media. Ben Jenkins explains in this recent interview.

Ben provides a smooth segue here to audio. All too often it's forgotten, and many marketers don't take advantage of another important tool.

Audio

The first thing that may come to mind for this category is podcasting. A **podcast** is a multimedia file available for downloading to an iPod, computer, or portable devices. Basically, a podcast is audio content typically hooked up to an RSS (really simple syndication) feed. Many associate only music with podcasting; however, there are many other applications.

Podcast novel reading in serial format is produced in episodes to capture and hold audiences. In the days of radio, vivid descriptions and interesting dialogue, stream of consciousness, music, and more held listeners in rapt attention. It wasn't arbitrarily referred to as "theater of the mind"; listeners had to imagine everything. Radio soap operas had a serial format and still do today on television. They end on a compelling "now what?" scene to tease you into watching them the next day. The formula seems to work well.

Podcast reading content ranges from classic to contemporary novels, and even unpublished authors. In addition, some blogs adopt an audio format. They can be riveting. There is also a wealth of music and host shows from which to choose. George Smyth (Electric Mix) has experimented with the format featuring new and up-and-coming bands who allow their music to be aired free of charge just to get their name and sound out there (http://glsmyth.com/Other/EMix/Music-Podcast/?Lesni_zver). Arrangements like Smyth and Electrix Mix's can produce payoffs in the way of creating a strong following or even recording contracts for unknown artists someone hears.

Podcasting seems to be good social media for a few general areas, including but not limited to religion, evangelists, politicians, and mainstream broadcasting. For example, NPR has a library of its more popular shows (*Car Talk, Planet Money*, and *Talk of the Nation*—to name three). To get a sense of some of the possibilities, go to NPR and you'll find it is deep with content and covers the map with everything from music to news, interviews, popular show features, and a lot more. Again, podcasting can be a powerful, flexible, and highly personal channel for social media (http://www.npr.org/rss/podcast/podcast_directory.php).

While RSS and the Atom standard are the main providers for major consumer feed readers, podcasts are another social network tool and have become a larger part of the marketing mix. Some wonderful applications may include a corporations' customer service via "how-to" or brand builders. Avon, John Deere, Southwest Airlines, and Whirlpool have used podcasting. Although audiences are smaller, they have a clear niche.

Listening

> "Listening is the single most valuable activity that you can engage in on the Social Web. As such, it's a great place to start your social media program. The Social Web is a place where you can learn about how every aspect of what you do is perceived, and then use that information to improve."
>
> Social Media Marketing—An Hour a Day—*Dave Evans*

Listening is an important component of social media marketing. If you initiate relevant conversations and have a good ear, you can learn a lot about your audience and what they really think—what they like and don't like about you, their recent experiences (good and bad) with your product or service, and if there's a buzz out there about you. In the latter instance, if something is amiss, listening can help put you in a preemptive mode. That's precisely what happened to Dave Shaunick, director of multichannel integration at a Sears Hometown Store in Dripping Springs, Texas, when he learned a deliveryman had accidentally run over a customer's dog.

Initial apologies were mishandled, but Shaunik and Sears business unit president Will Powell averted what might have escalated into a social media storm. They listened to the customer, assessed the problem, took what they felt was appropriate responsibility, apologized, and asked how Sears could "make it right." Their MO is detailed in the case study at http://stevefarnsworth. wordpress.com/2009/12/14/searskilledmydog-com-anatomy-social-media-nightmare-averted-%E2%80%93-a-case-study/.

Listening was the saving grace for Shaunik. He was *really* listening and responded quickly. Putting customers off and not revisiting the conversation in a timely fashion suggests a lack of concern. One of the biggest turn-offs consumers have about advertising in general is that it's a one-way conversation and doesn't speak to their needs. A real conversation includes listening, along with providing feedback to demonstrate you are listening.

Hearing isn't necessarily listening. Making an on-the-fly judgment or formulating an answer or reacting to what is being said isn't listening. When you are not listening, you are not learning. If you're not listening, you are missing out on some real opportunities. In social media you have a unique communications channel that gives you listening on a global scale. Rest assured that your customers are talking.

To a marketer, social networks are invaluable resources to stay abreast of how social communities perceive your company, service, or product. Understanding what your customers are thinking and saying helps you assess their needs. Having that information can help you engage your customer. What are they thinking? How do they feel about you? Having the answers to those questions can assist you better to shape creative strategy, formulate better ideas for solutions, and embrace the needs of your audience. Listening might seed promotions, contests, and engaging content. It may even provide an insight to product development.

That said, when listening, marketers should stay out of the conversation on social networks. Facebook, MySpace, and Twitter aren't broadcast media. They're engagement media. You don't want to be intrusive. To a marketer, social networks are good listening venues and provide invaluable resources to stay abreast of how your company, service, or product is doing. They are also good places to check out competitors. In crises or potential crises mode, listening can help a marketer be preemptive.

Listening can return rich rewards. It assists in establishing a healthy relationship with your audience while concurrently feeding a steady stream of information you can utilize to leverage an edge in your market. Ideally, listening will help reevaluate your approach to marketing from dominating the conversation to listening—and realizing it isn't all about you; it's about connecting with your customers and demonstrating you have been listening.

Bringing LeBron James to New York City—Despite the Knicks?

> "Our head of social media is the customer."
>
> —*McDonald's*

"C'mon LeBron" was an integrated campaign developed for NYC & Co. With tourism on the decline, New York City needed something to get people talking. Conveniently, at the same time the biggest sports figure on the planet, reigning basketball MVP LeBron James, was a free agent looking for a new home.

This offered BBH and Mark Svartz a unique perfect opportunity to give the people of New York a voice to show the world's greatest athlete why he belonged *there*—in the world's greatest city. All together, the entire campaign lasted less than a month. Here's the incredible part: It was accomplished for just $10,000 (most of which went toward printing T-shirts), but it got a lot of buzz.

Mark Svartz is a gifted artist, writer, and an award-winning advertising creative director, who has worked across media and produced ad campaigns for numerous blue chip clients. Some of them include Google Chrome, Sprite, New York Mets, Axe, Sprite, IBM, and Yahoo Music!

Currently, Svartz is working as a freelance creative director and copywriter.

He has worked at Ogilvy & Mather-NY and BBH-NY. His work has been recognized at Cannes, The One Show, *Communication Arts*, D&ED, National Addys, *Adweek's* "Best Spots," and TBS' America's Funniest Commercials.

As a writer and artist, Svartz offers insights on visual storytelling and social media in this recent interview.

The "C'mon LeBron" campaign is a fine example of how storytelling can be effectively integrated into visual storytelling. This ad outing—from start to finish—relied on its graphic power . . . much of which was created for and by its audience. How's that for efficient use of social media?

Social Networking, Advertising, and the Future

Actually, the concept of socialization is as old as civilization. At its base is our need to connect with others to share feelings, ideas, opinions, experience, and even expertise. Social networking nurtures friendships and grows communities of people who feel comfortable to share their daily lives with one another.

Anthony Ha has confidence in the effectiveness of social media in advertising. It's more than a trend, it's how Gen Y'ers and the Z'ers and whoever is next will likely be hanging out—for the foreseeable future, anyway. Here's his assessment from *AdWeek.com*. He notes four reasons why social networking is beginning to be able to contribute to revenues: more metrics, content is advertising is content, social blindness is less blind, and it's not just about Facebook.

> *More metrics.* Facebook says advertisers will soon be able to aim their messages at users even more carefully using data from Facebook's integration with media services like Spotify and Hulu. *Content is advertising is content.* Facebook and Twitter have both emphasized turning regular user content into ads—Facebook through its Sponsored Stories unit and Twitter through its Sponsored Tweets. *Social blindness less blind.* Some companies are working on ways to fight the clutter. Facebook, for instance, announced that it's starting to organize user newsfeeds based on an algorithm that it calls Graph Rank—so brand activity that's actually generating user interest won't get buried. *It's not just about Facebook.* The Pivot Conference found that 16 percent of respondents had run campaigns with Foursquare, and another 26 percent planned to do so in the next year. And *eMarketer* is projecting that LinkedIn's ad revenue will grow from $79 million last year to $250 million in 2013. (Ha, 2011)

Visual Communication and Being the Consumer

Ford Motor Company adopted an interesting advertising strategy that bridged into branding and social media with its "Fiesta Movement" campaign. The short version is that Ford locked onto its target—Gen Y'ers—for its Fiesta model, which fit the lifestyle, needs, and pocketbooks of that audience. The idea was that Ford would select 100 of 4,000 applicants to drive a Ford Fiesta for six months and share their experience with Ford and various social media sites and blogs. Again, Ford demonstrated a great deal of confidence in its product along with a sense of trust in the consumer—and potential customer. It's another great example of some of the smart, innovative thinking in marketing today: *Being like*, or at least thinking like, the consumer and realizing that the young Y-ers Ford is conversing with are more than potential customers: They're a growing, passionate group of culture creators.

Grant McCracken of *Harvard Business Review* agrees:

"Ford gave 100 consumers a car for six months and asked them to complete a different mission every month and away they went. At the direction of Ford and their own imagination, "agents" used their Fiestas to deliver Meals on Wheels. They used them to take Harry & David treats to the National Guard. They went looking for adventure, some to wrestle alligators, others actually to elope. All of these stories were then lovingly documented on YouTube, Flickr, Facebook, and Twitter" (McCracken, 2010).

Here's the other thing that brings us full circle—and back to appreciating and understanding how crucial graphic communication is to marketing: The Ford marketers knew the value of visual storytelling and how it couples up with social media. How else would their 100 lucky drivers best share their stories on YouTube, Facebook, and other social media venues? Show and tell won out once again. Tracy Wong knew this as well when he sought to bridge social media and sports culture by taking "GameDay" viewers behind the scenes and utilizing social media tools. Or convincing young people of the dangers of tobacco by letting them produce the content and ad peripherals for the "No Stank You" campaign. Ken Chitwood and Ben Jenkins of Sasquatch convinced Widmer Brewing that giving away craft beer recipes and taking their friends (consumers) backstage to the brewery and into a shared culture would resonate. Those craft beer drinkers won't forget either. From the looks of things, Frito-Lay and Doritos will continue to "Crash the Super Bowl," and football fans are wondering what will be next. Most of these folks were creating visual narratives that would create economic value—or really touch the hearts of people. Bill Bernbach would be proud.

References

Anderson, E. (2010). *Social media marketing: Game theory and the emergence of collaboration*. New York: Springer.

Aspray, W., & Campbell-Kelly, M. (1997). *Computer: A history of the information machine (Sloan Technology Series)*. New York: Basic.

British Broadcasting Corporation (BBC). (2011, February 17). Egypt: "We are all Khaled Said." *BBC World Service*. Retrieved from http://www.bbc.co.uk/worldservice/programmes/2011/02/110217_outlook_egypt_protests_khaled_said.shtml

Cohen, J. (2011, February 11). Google's Wael Ghonim thanks Facebook for revolution. *Allfacebook: The Unofficial Facebook Blog*. Retrieved from http://allfacebook.com/googles-wael-ghonim-thanks-facebook-for-revolution_b32315

Hansen, D., & Schneiderman, M. (2011). *Analyzing social media networks with NodeXL: Insights from a connected world*. Boston: Morgan Kaufman Publishers.

Indvik, L. (2001, October 9). How the 10 most popular Facebook brands rank by engagement. *Mashable Business*. Retrieved from http://mashable.com/2011/10/09/top-facebook-brands-talking-about/

Narins, B. (2001). *World of computer science*, Volume I. Belmont, CA: Thomson Gale.

Safko, L. (2012). *The social media bible: Tactics, tools, and strategies for business success*. New York: Wiley.

Social Media. (2012). Retrieved from http://en.wikipedia.org/wiki/Social_media#cite_note-Kietzmann_2011_241.E2.80.93251-1

SECTION 2
Evolving Media Issues

CHAPTER 5

Media, Sports and Evolving Forms of Entertaining

> When people fear for their futures, they like to gather in a dark room and stare at a screen, holding hands against the gloom.
>
> —*David Carr*

Consider the difference between the forms of entertainment you use every day and the sources of entertainment from a generation ago. Fifty years ago, people could only see movies in the theaters. But today, you have the option of going to the theater, watching movies on DVD or on-demand, or even downloading movies to your computer or iPod. Whereas your parents or grandparents would have gone to a stadium to watch a sporting event or listened to coverage of the event on the radio, you can turn to ESPN or watch videos on ESPN.com. And although your parents may have played early one- and two-player video games like "Pong," you now have the option of connecting with gamers worldwide via the Internet.

Entertainment is evolving. The motion picture industry, live theater, sports, newer mass media, such as video and online gaming, and popular theme parks mirror and comment on the larger society. The products created for these industries encapsulate slices of cultural history. They provide models for understanding the values and lifestyles in a culture. These media provide jobs and opportunities in art, communications, marketing, and advertising. It is important to understand the interactions between these media that can both define and reflect social trends. These are not news media, but they serve some of the same purposes as the news media.

Roles of the Entertainment Industry

The entertainment industries provide the public with information and entertainment, act as marketing tools, reflect changes in society, and satisfy our needs for communal activities. These roles are not entirely different from the roles of news media. And as we have discovered in our study of the "serious" mass media, the "fun" mass media—the entertainment industries—are being transformed by digital technologies at a very rapid rate. As these media are transformed, the interrelationship of the entertainment and news media grows.

Entertainment as Social Critique

The entertainment industries have become a prominent source of news, as new technologies, products, and business models provide vehicles to spread information. Entertainment productions bring up social issues such as gender, religion, bias, disease, crime, terrorism, and politics in myriad ways. In doing so, the entertainment industry helps inform, educate, and provoke discussion about these issues. Popular entertainment often pushes the envelope of what is socially acceptable.

Entertainment that produces discussion or controversy can energize people to take action in the real world. Interest groups or individuals frequently try to put pressure on legislators or regulators urging that media be censored or regulated due to its perceived negative effects on society.

The Southern Baptist Convention (SBC) ended an eight-year boycott of Disney parks in 2005. The SBC boycott was aimed at ending Disney's policy of extending benefits to homosexual employees and sponsorship of "Gay Days." The boycott had no discernable financial impact on corporate policy and ended when Disney studios and Miramax films split up.

Fines and threats have led to networks choosing censorship. Popular controversial radio host Howard Stern's move from public broadcast radio to subscription satellite radio was motivated in part by his reaction to FCC fines and his network's attempts to tone down his program.

The Entertainment Software Rating Board (ESRB) was started by electronic game companies to head off government regulation of violent or sexually explicit content in games. The game rating system is modeled on the Motion Picture Association of America (MPAA) movie ratings.

Information about each of the rating systems and how these ratings should help parents and others in guiding entertainment choices for children and teens is carefully detailed by the American Academy of Pediatricians (AAP). According to the AAP:

> Ratings have become more common because research has shown how much children are influenced by what they see and hear, especially at very young ages. The effects don't seem to go away as the child gets older. One study of 8-year-old boys found that those who watched violent TV programs growing up were most likely to be involved in aggressive, violent behavior by age 18 and serious criminal behavior by age 30 (American Academy of Pediatrics, 2001).

Motion Picture Industry: From Pictures to Pixels

The film industry is subject to a wave of changes in how it creates, produces, markets, and distributes its creative content. Today, movies are made available to the public in theaters, on DVD, and online.

Hollywood's "Golden Age"

In the early days of motion pictures, studios and movie theaters operated independently. As the industry matured, the studios moved to acquire control beyond the ownership of the talent, production facilities, and titles. They began to purchase movie theaters, from small town cinemas to grand movie palaces. This is called vertical integration because one company controls a product from its inception to its final form.

Vertical integration enables a movie studio to set prices and policies from top to bottom. Actors, directors, writers, producers, and theater owners depend upon large consolidated studios for work. They also depend on these studios to distribute their work to audiences.

From its beginnings, Hollywood movie production moved toward consolidation. By the 1930s, Warner Bros., Paramount, 20th Century Fox, Loew's (MGM), and RKO (Radio-Keith-Orpheum) were the major players and had achieved vertical integration. Along with "The Little Three"—Universal, Columbia, and United Artists—these companies operated as a mature oligopoly. Eight companies essentially controlled the entire market.

When their films came out, the studios took advantage of their vertical integration to force independent theaters to do block booking, where popular films were paired with B-list films that the theaters had to accept and screen, often sight unseen, as part of the deal.

In the 1940s, independent movie producers and exhibitors challenged the monopolistic behavior of the major studios. In the 1948 case *U.S. v. Paramount Pictures*, the studios were ordered to divest themselves of their theaters. The studios complied and this opened up the market. However with the post-war boom in television beginning in 1950, the economic model that had prevailed in the movie industry since the 1930s was further disrupted.

Hollywood's "Golden Age," when those eight companies had control of 95 percent of all film rentals and close to 70 percent of all box-office receipts, came to an end. There are parallels between those "Golden" days and today. Hollywood and the movies went through a difficult time when many predicted the demise of movies in the face of the "new media" of that time—broadcast television.

It is ironic that the "Big Three" television corporations, ABC, CBS, and NBC, established near-monopolistic control of television broadcasting only to face similar challenges with the rise of cable television and expansion of the number of channels available for programming.

Current Trends and the Impact of Technology

Current trends in entertainment include the rapid growth of video on demand and availability of television content on various kinds of digital playback devices, such as cell phones and iPods. Although unsettled and still in search of economically viable business models, these trends are further transforming the television industry. However, this move to unbundle content from any particular method of delivery is perceived as a threat by the movie industry. The motion picture industry lobbies Congress to "dumb down" playback devices and add "flags" and other copy-protection to some forms of content in an attempt to shore up analog business models in a digital world.

Meanwhile, technology continues to improve other parts of the movie industry. New digital formats designed for theater use can make the viewing experience more realistic, as HDTV is doing in living rooms everywhere. Re-fitting theaters with new projectors and sound systems is costly. The theater owners must find the appropriate price that an audience will be willing to pay for a better viewing experience in order to make the transition to digital projection systems work.

The Bureau of Labor Statistics notes that:

Most motion pictures are still made on film. However, digital technology and computer-generated imaging are rapidly making inroads and are expected to transform the industry . . . Digital technology also makes it possible to distribute movies to theaters through the use of satellites or fiber-optic cable. Bulky metal film canisters can be replaced by easy-to-transport hard drives, although relatively few theaters are capable of receiving and screening movies in that manner now. In the future, however, more theaters will be capable of projecting films digitally and the costly process of producing and distributing films will be sharply reduced (Bureau of Labor Statistics, U.S. Department of Labor, 2009a).

This is causing major concern throughout the movie business. The move to digital production and projection means new methods of making pictures. Old jobs will be replaced by new ones to suit digital movie making. The entire industry needs to re-tool its equipment across production, distribution, and presentation in the transition to digital media.

Disney, Fox, MGM, Paramount, Sony Pictures Entertainment, Universal, and Warner Bros. Studios created Digital Cinema Initiatives in March 2002 to " . . . establish and document voluntary specifications for an open architecture for digital cinema that ensures a uniform and high level of technical performance, reliability, and quality control" (Digital Cinema Initiatives, LLC, 2008).

Theater owners fear the expense of the changeover. Audiences would appreciate better images, but may resist higher box office prices. The Screen Actors Guild (SAG) has spoken out about actors receiving fair compensation for movies and television shows that are sold and downloaded onto iPods. In 2006, SAG president Alan Rosenberg accused ABC of selling *Lost* and *Desperate Housewives* for digital download to iPods without first bargaining with the Screen Actors Guild. ABC intends to pay residuals to performers based on the videocassette formula, which SAG doesn't believe is fair. SAG is going to take action to challenge ABC's decision.

Directors have to adapt their vision to the new medium. In the analog world, television and motion pictures were different media and each had its own aesthetic. From crew to cast to director and writers, working in the movies was similar but not identical to working in television. When "filming" a production or live event happens digitally, what is left to distinguish a motion picture from a television show or even from a news package? The resulting product is a set of moving images that have been recorded, edited, and packaged in a digital medium. Is it a film when it isn't captured on filmstock? Is it television if it's a movie that can be played back equally well in a theater, on a television set, or on a computer screen?

Compensation Changes

What kind of compensation will content producers receive when a work can be viewed on many platforms and the viewer has control over the medium for viewing? This question is debatable, but we can look at how the music recording and radio industries worked out similar issues involving analog recording.

In an era when pre-recorded music was becoming a staple of radio, musicians, composers, radio stations and networks faced fundamental changes in operations. This gave rise to disputes about fees and residuals. In 1914, Tin Pan Alley songwriters joined up with the American Society of Composers and Publishers (ASCAP), whose function was to set up and collect royalties each time a licensed song was played. Initially, most of the revenue ASCAP collected was generated by the sale of sheet music, variety shows, dance band programs, and the like that aired on radio. Later, prerecorded music became the biggest source of ASCAP's revenues.

Photography as a Communication Channel

We live in an increasingly visual culture. In the early part of the 21st century, video seems to be the most dominant force in the entertainment industry.

The modern "picture press" began in 1842 with the *Illustrated London News*, taking a form we recognize as modern after World War I. Public interest in stories told with pictures, the brief rise of a free press in Germany after the war, and technology in the form of small, light, easy-to-use cameras gave rise to more printed photos.

World War II was the impetus that drove many European photographers and photo editors to emigrate to the United States. They gathered in New York City where Henry Luce ran the publishing empire that included *Life*, a showcase for photographers from advertising and journalism. The picture story captured the American imagination at the same time that it helped form America's idea of itself and present its face to the world.

Many modern photographers, such as Margaret Bourke-White and Edward Steichen, produced photographs we regard as art, as well as journalistic and advertising images. In the 1930s, these photographers, as well as filmmakers and writers, began to work in a style called documentary. These types of works looked with a critical eye at social issues such as poverty and injustice. Writer and critic Walter Benjamin made the distinction between an art photo without a news caption and "responsible image making." The art photo can transform poverty or pain into something beautiful to behold, but the photographer uses words to anchor the photo's meaning to the real world.

In the pre-television era before World War II, people read pictorial magazines eagerly and these magazines flourished in major cities around the world. The stories in these magazines became the narratives that helped create national consciousness in countries that had been wracked by war. The popularity and growth in the number of magazines that featured photo stories made it easy for photographers to become freelancers and leave their jobs at publishing houses. The independence of freelancers from strict editorial directives led to an era of creative, individualistic work.

During the 1950s and 60s, photographic images in narrative stories and advertising were one of the most influential mass media. However, the increasing availability of television, and especially the Vietnam War, began to draw viewers away from print to the television screen.

The large national magazines such as *Look* and *Life* couldn't compete with the six o'clock news and the visceral imagery of the ongoing casualties and process of the war. Color television became ubiquitous and was hungry for images that moved viewers.

The influential image-makers began to work in television and the movies. Theaters and TV sets became the primary media through which audiences were exposed to images.

Live Performance: From Theater to Touring

Theater is intertwined with American history. Like any mass medium, live theater entertains, educates, and mirrors society. Theater in the United States was star-driven when it began. Theater companies had their own playhouses in cities and towns across the country. They developed a set of plays to showcase their stars. As conditions shifted economically, and other mass media underwent some changes, live theater production changed as well.

Broadway

A collaborative system arose where a producer and director assembled a team including writers, actors, and stage designers to produce a play that would hopefully have a long, successful run on the theater circuit. These productions were typically large scale and often began on Broadway before moving out of New York to other cities and regional theaters.

By the 1960s, the heyday of Broadway was over. Playwrights from Chicago, Los Angeles, and other cities were writing plays that were produced outside New York. August Wilson, David Huang, Wendy Wasserstein, Des McAnuff, David Mamet, Tony Kushner, and Peter Sellars were a few of the playwrights of the time. For them, New York is an important place to show off their work, but it isn't the ultimate destination. Theater is alive and well in the United States these days, though there are fewer theaters and performances going on today than there were in the 1900s. At that time, there were fewer other media to compete with live theater for an audience.

Today, Broadway features are often based on books or movies that were bestsellers or blockbusters. A success on Broadway frequently leads to a movie version for popular plays and musicals.

Synergy: Developing Conglomerates

Large media corporations look for what they call synergy in entertainment properties. In the 1980s, businesses began to grow by combining with other businesses into conglomerates. A single corporate entity would consist of many smaller businesses that did not all specialize in the same commercial enterprise.

For example, suppose a corporation purchases the rights to a good book. That book can then be adapted for screen and stage, be made into a show or ride at a theme park, or perhaps spawn an electronic game. As a result, these ventures would drive the market for retail merchandise such as dolls, toys, and costumes. That's synergy at work. The synergy builds additional opportunities for profit for large corporations from a single entertainment property.

Disney's "The Lion King," "Beauty and the Beast," and "Mulan" are examples of this type of corporate undertaking. The entertainment products include picture books, coloring books, videos, films, lavish traveling musicals, shows at ice arenas, and features at theme parks.

New Mass Media Entertainment: Can We Have Your Attention, Please?

Theme parks, sports, and electronic games represent new kinds of mass media that have been attracting growing audiences and experiencing revenue growth since the 1970s.

Theme Parks

The Disney theme parks are an important part of the corporate focus on synergy and creating demand for its entertainment products inside and outside the gates of the theme park. Disney remained the top chain, with 116.5 million visitors worldwide last year, followed by Merlin Entertainment with 32.1 million. Universal drew 26.4 million, followed by Six Flags with 24.9 million and Busch with 22.3 million. Cedar Fair came in sixth place, with 22.1 million visitors in 2007 (ThemeParkInsider, 2008).

Sports

When the Entertainment and Sports Programming Network (ESPN) launched the first all-sports cable channel on September 7, 1979, its success was by no means a sure thing. Bill Rasmussen, formerly a semi-pro hockey team's PR man, fought to create the network, using Getty Oil money to get it off the ground. In its early years, ESPN wasn't profitable. With a limited budget and no connections to major sports programming, ESPN was forced to carry rarely watched sporting events.

Unable to afford to carry football, baseball, or any of the other major sports, ESPN concentrated its efforts on its news programming. This proved to be a wise decision.

ESPN put its resources into its news show, Sportscenter, and network executives turned college basketball games and the National Football League draft into television events. They made masterful use of marketing and built audiences for sports television in new ways. By 1995, ESPN was the first cable network to make it into 70 percent of homes in the United States. By 2005, ESPN had surpassed 90 million households. Currently it is available in more than 98 million homes (http://www.espnmediazone.com/corp_info/corp_fact_sheet.html).

ESPN's properties include ESPN, ESPN2, ESPN Classic Sports, ESPNews and ESPN The Magazine. ESPN Original Entertainment has developed the sports game show "ESPN's 2-Minute Drill" and the documentary "The Season" and continues to create new sports-based programming.

Old Media: Going Digital

Global spending on entertainment media dipped in 2000 after the dotcom boom but has steadied and was expected to reach $690 billion by 2009 (http://paidcontent.org/article/419-global-internet-spending-expected-to-rise-107-percent-annually-through-/). Demand for digital distribution of music, books, films, and video games is increasing.

The availability of high speed broadband is a major catalyst behind this trend according to industry analysts. Threats to growth in entertainment industries lurk in rising interest rates and skyrocketing energy costs. The demand for this kind of entertainment is increasing in developing countries, particularly China. This pressure will continue to increase overall spending on these media.

The recession will last longer than previous ones due to a steeper downturn and the impact on consumer spending will be much steeper than in the past, but spending on entertainment and media will continue to grow. Video games, online film rentals, digital distribution of music, music for mobile devices, e-books, video on demand, and satellite radio spending will grow by 2.7 per cent compounded annually for the entire forecast period to $1.6 trillion in 2013. The spending will likely see a 3.9 per cent drop in 2009 and a mere 0.4 per cent advance in 2010, with a period of much faster growth of about seven per cent in 2013. Video games, online film rentals, digital distribution of music, music for mobile devices, e-books, video on demand, and satellite (subscription) radio accounted for about $160 million in 2000. By 2004, this had risen to $11.4 billion (http://www.pwc.com/gx/en/press-room/2009/global-entertain-and-media-outlook-2009.jhtml).

As demand for the electronic forms of media grows, sales of physical media continue to fall. Physical music (such as CDs), home video rentals, and PC games are examples of content that can be delivered as physical or electronic media. Increasingly, consumers favor electronic delivery.

Electronic Games

In the 1970s and 80s, arcade games like "Pac-Man" and "Pong" by Atari were popular in bars and restaurants. In 1972, Magnavox introduced the Odyssey game console that connected to a television set and played "Pong." The Odyssey system came with "Pong" but its program cards were removable like modern game systems such as Xbox and PlayStation.

The system was primitive by today's standards, but over 80,000 units were sold in 1972. Another 250,000-plus Odyssey machines were sold between 1973 and late 1975, bringing the total to over 350,000 units sold. The system was removed from stores in late 1975 and replaced by a newer, simpler model: the Odyssey 100. As simple as it was, the Odyssey set the stage for increasingly sophisticated game boxes and online games such as the massive multi-player "World of Warcraft."

In 2005, video games brought in a record $10.5 billion in sales of hardware, software, and accessories (http://www.foxnews.com/story/0,2933,181816,00.html). Electronic games played on "game boxes" were initially connected to video outputs and limited to players who were together in time and space. "Mario Bros," "Pong," "Donkey Kong," and games of this generation had colorful animations and catchy background music loops. Players took turns competing against characters in the game.

Multiple player games were developed so that several players could compete against each other and against the game. Before the World Wide Web and broadband, there were a variety of games that allowed players to compete with one another online. The history of these games goes back to the time before the World Wide Web when text-based games such as "Zork" and "StarTrek" were played via CRTs (cathode ray tubes), using mainframe computers.

The number of these games has expanded since the 1990s. Many of them now have fan web sites that provide information about the games, fan art, and discussion forums. Some sites even include video and audio "mash-ups," in which fans use images from screengrabs and audio from the games to create their own videos and MP3s.

U.S. consumer spending on online games jumped about 20 percent from $73 million in 2003 to $88.8 million in 2004 and $54.4 million for the first half of 2005. It is projected that U.S. in-game advertising spending will increase from $295 million in 2007 to $650 million in 2012 (http://www. emarketer.com/Reports/All/Emarketer_2000485.aspx). Spending for online games is expected to climb higher throughout the decade.

The attraction of these worlds is based on their interactivity and the way they evolve into social communities. With each improvement in computer graphics or broadband speed, the games become more entertaining and sophisticated.

Although they are different than traditional entertainments that occur face-to-face in the real world, such as sporting events, concerts, or plays, the pleasure and problems of virtual entertainments appear to be no better or worse than traditional entertainments.

And the Future Will Bring . . .

Studies of people in their teens indicate that they are heavy users of all media, which is not surprising. However, the degree to which teens multi-task—for example, watch television while they type a paper on their computers and instant message with friends—represents something new in mass media. Media professionals who must connect with people to get their message across, whether it is news, entertainment or advertising, say we are in an "attention economy."

The message doesn't just need to get into the media; it has to break through a barrage of media to capture someone's attention. When individuals had fewer choices in mass media, media producers could better serve as the information gatekeepers who controlled what the viewers or listeners could tune in to, and when. Times have changed.

Analog technologies that made it difficult to combine content from different media are easier to work around and are being replaced in a world of digital information. The public audience is no longer a bunch of passive consumers. They are media makers, the editors and program directors in the "Me Media" environment today.

What lies ahead for mass media entertainment? More choices, more user control, more competition for attention and hopefully more fun as the existing businesses and industries adapt to our digital century or go out of style!

References

American Academy of Pediatrics. (2001). *Entertainment rating system—Why it was developed*. Retrieved from http://www.medem.com/medlib/article/ZZZRI81PASD

Bureau of Labor Statistics, U.S. Department of Labor. (2009a). *Career guide to industries, 2008–09 edition: Motion picture and video industries*. Retrieved from http://www.bls.gov/oco/cg/cgs038.htm

Bureau of Labor Statistics, U.S. Department of Labor. (2009b). *Career guide to industries, 2008–09 edition: Arts, entertainment, and recreation*. Retrieved from http://www.bls.gov/oco/cg/cgs031.htm

Digital Cinema Initiatives, LLC. (2008). *About DCI*. Retrieved from http://www.dcimovies.com/

ThemeParkInsider. (March 14, 2008). *"2007 theme park attendance report released" by Robert Niles*. Retrieved from http://www.themeparkinsider.com/flume/200803/649/

CHAPTER 6

Evolving Media Issues: Video Game Violence

"Distracted from distraction by distraction"

—*T. S. Eliot*

Not unlike the Internet and cell phones, video games are such a significant part of our popular culture that it is hard to imagine a time before they existed. With their initial reputation as a novelty or a toy in the early 1970s, video games quickly expanded into a multi-billion-dollar industry by the mid-1980s (Wolf, 2001), and the popularity of video game entertainment has continued to rise over the past few years. In 2010, the game industry reaped colossal profits of more than $20 billion in the U.S. Goldberg (2011) reports that 77% of households play video games, and people are now spending more money on video games than on music, movies, and DVDs, lending support to the suggestion that video game play is displacing other media use (Slocombe, 2005).

While popular commentary about video game violence rages, we have yet to answer the question: Do violent video games cause aggression, do those who already have violent tendencies choose to play games with aggressive themes, or are video games simply a reflection of our culture's fascination with and glorification of violence? Recent research suggests that there may be a connection between game play and aggressive tendencies. At the same time, specific types of content may have a stronger impact on game players in terms of aggression, as may the extent to which game players adapt to their environment.

Violent Video Games and User Responses

The gradual increase in video game use across the U.S. has led policymakers and researchers to consider its effects on attitudes, behaviors, and beliefs. In a study of game players' usage habits, Sherry, Lucas, Greenberg, and Lachlan (2006) found that children, adolescents, and adults of both sexes spend a substantial amount of time playing video games. On average, males in their early teens spend about 11 hours playing console games every week. Most American households have at least one game console, with about a third of these game consoles located in bedrooms or other places where game play goes unmonitored (Kaiser Family Foundation, 1999).

Both casual observation and scientific research (see below) indicate that video games contain lots of violence and aggression. As video games have become more sophisticated over the years (think about how different *Frogger* and *Halo* are in terms of realism), these portrayals of violence have become faster paced, more graphic, and more realistic. A number of early studies tried to tie together game play and aggressive attitudes or worldviews (Dominick, 1984). Wiegman and Van Shie (1998) found that children who played video games more often were identified by their classmates as more aggressive. Similar correlations between video game play and aggressive tendencies have been reported in studies looking at both children (Dominick, 1984; Lin & Lepper, 1987) and adults (Anderson & Dill, 2000).

While these studies are informative and offer some evidence of a link between game play and aggression, they are based on self-reports and evaluation by others, as well as other loosely linked factors. In other words, while we can say that there is a link here, these studies don't give us any reason to believe that game play *causes* aggression. Fortunately, a number of experimental studies have explored the causal link between video game play and aggression, at least in terms of short term responses. Anderson and Ford (1986), Ballard and Lineberger (1999), Anderson and Dill (2000), and others have looked at actual behaviors following game play. They have found that when provoked, adults who have just played a violent video game are more likely to do rather unpleasant things to others when given the opportunity. These include administering long, loud blasts of obnoxious noise, or forcibly immersing someone's hand in ice-cold water. While it is scientifically unethical to conduct studies such as these with children, there are a few less severe studies that indicate a causal relationship between video game play and aggression among kids. For example, Shutte, Malouf, Post-Gordon, and Rodasta (1987) exposed seven-year olds to either a violent or a non-violent video game. When given a chance for "free play" with a Bobo doll, the children who played the violent game were more likely to abuse the Bobo doll or to *attack each other* than were those playing the nonviolent game.

Telepresence, the Feeling of "Being There"

The notion that there is some kind of connection—be it a correlation or a causal link—between video game play and aggression is clearly not a new one. There have, however, been some new developments in our thinking over the last 10 years or so. Sherry (2001) published what researchers call a meta-analysis, or a mathematical evaluation of all of the major studies that have been published linking video games and aggression. This study revealed that, among other things, the strength of the relationship between game playing and aggression is increasing over time. In other words, the newer the study, the stronger the link between the two. This has led researchers to start thinking about how video games may have changed over the decades, and the ways in which these changes may impact subsequent responses by game players. Put another way: *Why is this relationship stronger than it used to be?*

Obviously, video games have changed in terms of their realism, intensity, and graphicness. Simple graphic representations of tanks and missiles as crude squares on a green background have been replaced by life-like, three dimensional avatars, advanced artificial intelligence, realistic interactions, and competitive game play environments against other gamers. These realistic game environments may lead to a psychological experience known as *telepresence,* in which game players feel as though they have left their physical world and have become immersed in a mediated one. At this point, a sense of separation from the "real world" breaks down, and people may be more likely to respond to mediated characters as though they were real, and they may also be more likely to acquire attitudes, beliefs, and action tendencies from their reactions to these characters.

Lombard and Ditton (1997) define presence as "a psychological state or subjective perception in which even though part or all of an individual's current experience is generated by and/or filtered through human-made technology, part or all of the individual's perception fails to accurately acknowledge the role of the technology in the experience" (Lombard, 2000, cited in Bracken, 2006, p. 725). Steuer (1992) and others argue that situational factors related to the game user, such as the level of experience with the medium and general aptitude at adapting to mediated environments, may also play a role in the level of presence one experiences, and the degree to which one may acquire attitudes and action tendencies. It is not difficult to see that video games are far more complex and realistic than they used to be, and that individuals are spending more time with video games than they have in the past. If this is the case, then people may be becoming more adept at these complex interactions, and more susceptible to learning aggressive thoughts and scripts from them.

A study by Tamborini, Eastin, Skalski, Lachlan, Fediuk, & Brady (2004) has offered at least initial evidence of this type of process. In this particular study, participants were assigned to play or to observe violent and non-violent video games. The results revealed that participants experienced higher levels of presence when playing, as opposed to watching video game play. They also discovered that those observing a non-violent game were found to express less hostility when provoked than those playing or watching a violent game. While the connections here are somewhat loose, they do suggest that presence may play a role in whether or not video game play leads to subsequent aggression.

Thinking about Video Game Content

In addition to concerns regarding the experience of presence and realism, scholars have also turned their attention to the specific types of violence we can expect in video games, how often they occur, who is involved, and what this violence looks like. In one of the earliest studies of this kind, Braun and Giroux (1989) evaluated 21 arcade games in an attempt to figure out how often violence takes place. They observed that roughly three quarters of the games they looked at featured death or destruction of some kind; not surprisingly, games with themes related to war or crime were more likely to feature this kind of content. A number of years later, Haninger and Thompson (2004) examined "T" rated games, in order to get an idea of the violence in kids' games and what kind of violence might happen deeper into the games. They found that about 90% of the games required the use of violence, while 69% required the killing of other game characters.

While these studies provide useful data, they fail to acknowledge the specific contexts in which video game violence may occur. This is problematic, given decades of research in other media suggesting that certain types of violence may be more or less likely to engender aggressive responses in viewers. Of note, much of the research in film violence suggests that violence that is rewarded, justified, committed with weapons, repetitive in nature, graphic, committed by liked characters, or committed by attractive characters may be especially powerful as behavioral models that people will want to imitate. Given this knowledge, Smith, Lachlan, and Tamborini (2003) looked at the ways in which these context elements changed across games rated for different age groups, as well as the relative frequency of violent interactions in these contexts. Looking at the top 60 games from the 1999 calendar year, they identified individual acts of violence and their context, using the coding scheme from the National Television Violence Study. They found that games rated for mature audiences featured an average of 4.59 acts of violence per minute, over four times the rate found on television. Further, the context of violence in games rated for these audiences was cause for concern, as violence in these games was more likely to repeat violence, gun violence, and bloodshed and gore.

The authors published a number of follow-up studies, looking at the same data in different ways. One study revealed that gun violence is rampant in video games (Smith, Lachlan, Pieper, Boyson, Wilson, Tamborini, & Weber, 2004). Of equal concern, this gun violence is typically presented alongside other problematic contextual features. These include a lack of realism, justification for the violent act, and repetitive gun violence that may systematically desensitize.

A second follow-up study looked at the physical attributes of violent game characters, since past research evidence has shown that people are more likely to model behavior after individuals they find attractive or perceive as similar to themselves (Lachlan, Smith, & Tamborini, 2005). This study revealed that violent game perpetrators are often presented as white males, and it adds that video games are especially popular with white male adolescents. When looking at the results across these three studies, a concerning picture begins to emerge. The world of video games, according to these data, is full of repetitive violence, violence that frequently involves guns, and violence committed by characters that look like the people who are most commonly playing the games.

While the studies by Braun and Giroux, Haninger and Thompson, and Lachlan and colleagues are valuable, they overlook some of the nuances of video game play. As stated earlier, the experience of presence is likely to have an impact on game play experiences, as is the psychological makeup of the individual game player. Experience playing a particular game or video games in general may mitigate the decisions one makes in a virtual environment, as may one's general level of comfort ability with interactivity. These content studies are based on analytic techniques that were developed for linear media, such as television and film, and may not lend themselves all that well to interactive media such as video games (Schmierbach, 2010). Fortunately, there is one study in the literature that has attempted to address some of these concerns.

Lachlan and Maloney (2008) attempted to take a first look at the relationship between game player attributes and aggressive content. In a sense, they decided to look at how video game violence would manifest itself in decisions made by game players within the interactive environment. The authors randomly assigned a large number of game players (160) to a small number of games (4), to see how content would change from player to player depending on these attributes and experiences. They found that the frequency of violence and the context in which it might be found varied greatly from player to player. They also found that certain player attributes predicted violent behavior in the game, and that these causes were not the same from game to game.

In some games, physical aggressiveness and argumentativeness predicted certain types of violent acts, while in others psychoticism or vigilateism positively predicted the number of certain violent acts. Across all games, experienced presence *negatively predicted gun violence.* In fact, across the board, presence was negatively associated with violent acts of all kinds. At first glance, this seems to contradict our earlier reasoning about the relationship between immersive experiences and aggression. Lachlan and Maloney (2008), however, offer an alternate viewpoint on these processes, and one that begs us to look deeper into the interactive nature of video game violence.

While not formally measured in their study, Lachlan and Maloney, along with their research assistants, noted that just because someone committed a lot of violence did not mean that the person was doing it well. In examining tape recordings of the game play, they noticed that there were a number of players who didn't grasp the game very well and proverbially "shot at everything that moved."

Game players that struggled to navigate the game environment often sprayed off dozens of rounds of ammunition in no particular direction. By contrast, those that seemed to adapt well to the interactive environment actually committed fewer acts of violence. This is because they knew how to use aggressive acts to accomplish goals, such as killing enemies, destroying buildings, and moving on to more advanced levels of the game.

This observation forces us to question our real concerns about the nature of violent video game content and its effects on attitudes, behaviors, and beliefs. While media scientists have traditionally thought of violence in very simple "more = bad" terms, this picture may be incomplete. Should we be concerned about the game player who staggers around not knowing what he is doing, or the game player who very methodically knows how to kill in order to accomplish goals? The instrumental nature of violence has gone relatively unexamined in the video game literature, and its consideration is essential if we are to further disentangle the relationship between violent game play and subsequent aggressive attitudes and behaviors.

Bearing in mind the standing that video games occupy culturally, it cannot be ignored that social effects are present. Research indicates there is a small, but significant, overall effect of video game play on aggression, and this effect is positively related to the *type* of game violence (Sherry, 2001). That is, realistic, sanitized, justified, humorous, and rewarded violent acts committed by an attractive or similar looking character are linked to greater effects on aggression than violence that is unwarranted and fantastical and that results in negative consequences or punishments. Additionally, certain video game genres tend to be more violent and can have greater effects on aggression. First-person shooter, fighting, action, and adventure games are often more violent and have a tendency to reward players with points, bonus rounds, new weapons, and extra lives for carrying out the most brutal acts imaginable.

The development of technological innovations, such as high-definition game graphics, surround sound, accelerometers, increased processing speed, rumble features, on-controller speakers, touch screens, improved hard-drive memory, and more naturally mapped controllers are increasingly immersing media users in interactive worlds of violence. With these advancements in intensity and graphicness of video games, children will have trouble distinguishing between reality and fantasy and could easily be influenced by the images, characters, and scenarios on the screen (Villani, Olson & Jellinek, 2005).

The fact that many of the most popular video games contain violent themes has people debating whether the effects on attitudes, behaviors, and beliefs can be attributed to intrinsic or extrinsic factors. Does exposure to a perpetual diet of video game violence and hostility make people more aggressive, or are naturally aggressive people more drawn to violent content? This chicken-or-egg conundrum deserves further exploration, and additional research on the interactive nature of video game violence is essential to our understanding of the impacts and consequences of this ever-evolving technology. Furthermore, continued research in this area can help shed light on real world problems and concerns. As parents, teachers, and policymakers become increasingly concerned with the impact of video games on physcial and psychological health, this research can help us determine the types of content that are problematic, the extent to which they are problematic, and the role that the skills and personalities of individual game players play in this whole process. Armed with this body of knowledge, parernts may be able to make better decisions about buying games for their kids, policymakers may be better able to suggest rating and content management guidelines, and game players may become more aware of the effects that their own gaming may have on them.

References

Anderson, C. A., & Dill, K. E. (2000). Video games and aggressive thoughts, feelings, and behavior in the laboratory and in life. *Journal of Personality and Social Psychology, 78,* 772–790.

Anderson, C. A., & Ford, C. M. (1986). Affect of the game player: Short-term effects of highly and mildly aggressive video games. *Personality and Social Psychology Bulletin, 12,* 390–402.

Ballard, M. E., & Lineberger, R. (1999). Video game violence and confederate gender: Effects on reward and punishment given by college males. *Sex Roles, 41,* 541–558.

Bracken, C. C. (2006). Perceived source credibility of local television news: The impact of television form and presence. *Journal of Broadcasting and Electronic Media, 50,* 723–741.

Braun, C. M. J., & Giroux, J. (1989). Arcade video games: Proxemic, cognitive, and content analyses. *Journal of Leisure Research, 21,* 92–105.

Dietz, T. (1998). An examination of violence and gender role portrayals in video games: Implications for gender socialization and aggressive behavior. *Sex Roles, 38,* 425–442.

Dominick, J. R. (1984). Videogames, television violence, and aggression in teenagers. *Journal of Communication, 34,* 136–147.

Goldberg, H. (2011). *All your base are belong to us: How fifty years of videogames conquered pop culture.* New York: Three Rivers Press.

Haninger, K., & Thompson, K.M. (2004). Content and ratings of teen-rated video games. *Journal of the American Medical Association, 291* (7), 856–865.

Kaiser Family Foundation (1999). *Kids & media @ the new millennium: A comprehensive national analysis of children's media use.* Menlo Park, CA: Kaiser Family Foundation.

Lachlan, K.A., & Maloney, E.K. (2008). Game player characteristics and interactive content: Exploring the role of personality and telepresence in video game violence. *Communication Quarterly, 56* (3), 284–302.

Lachlan, K.A., Smith, S.L., & Tamborini, R. (2005). Models for aggressive behavior: The attributes of violent characters in popular video games. *Communication Studies, 56* (4), 313–329.

Lin, S., & Lepper, M. R. (1987). Correlates of children's usage of videogames and computers. *Journal of Applied Social Psychology, 17,* 72–93.

Lombard, M. (2000). *The concept of presence: Explication statement.* Available online at http://www.temple.edu/ispr/index.htm. Retrieved July 16, 2011.

Lombard, M. & Ditton, T. (1997). At the heart of it all: The concept of presence. *Journal of Computer Mediated Communication, 3*(2). Retrieved July 27, 2011, from http://www.ascusc.org/jcmc/vol3/issue2/lombard.html.

Schmierbach, M. (2010). Content analysis of video games: Challenges and potential solutions. *Communication Methods and Measures, 3,* 147–171.

Sherry, J. (2001). The effects of violent video games on aggression: A meta-analysis. *Human Communication Research, 27,* 409–431.

Sherry, J., Lucas, K., Greenberg, B.S., & Lachlan, K.A. (2006). Video game uses and gratifications as predictors of use and game preference. In P. Vorderer and J. Bryant (Eds.), *Playing computer games: Motives, responses, and consequences.* Cresskill, NJ: LEA.

Shutte, N. S., Malouf, J. M., Post-Gordon, J. C., & Rodasta, A. L. (1987). Effects of playing videogames on children's aggressive and other behaviors. *Journal of Applied Social Psychology, 18,* 454–460.

Slocombe, M. (2005). Men spend more money on video games than music: Nielsen report. *Digital-Lifestyles.* Available online at: http://digitallifestyles.info/display_page.asp?section=cm&id=2091. Retrieved July 30, 2011.

Smith, S. L., Lachlan, K. A., & Tamborini, R. (2003). Popular video games: Quantifying the presentation of violence and its context. *Journal of Broadcasting and Electronic Media, 47,* 58–76.

Smith, S. L., Lachlan, K. A., Pieper, K. M., Boyson, A. R. Wilson, B. J., Tamborini, R., & Weber, R. (2004). Brandishing guns in American Media: Two studies examining how often and in what context firearms appear on television and in popular video games. *Journal of Broadcasting and Electronic Media, 48* (4), 584–606.

Steuer, J. (1992). Defining virtual reality: Dimensions determining telepresence. *Journal of Communication, 42,* 73–93.

Tamborini, R., Eastin, M., Skalski, P. D., Lachlan, K. A., Fediuk, T., & Brady, R. (2004). Violent virtual video games and hostile thoughts. *Journal of Broadcasting and Electronic Media, 48,* 335–357.

Villani, V.S., Olson, C.K. & Jellinek, M.S. (2005). Media literacy for clinicians and parents. *Child and Adolescent Psychiatric Clinics of North America, 14,* 523–553.

Wiegman, O., & Van Shie, E. G. M. (1998). Video game playing and its relations with aggressive and prosocial behavior. *British Journal of Social Psychology, 37,* 367–378.

Wolf, M. J. P. (2001). Space in the video game. In M. J. P. Wolf (Ed.), *The medium of the videogame* (pp. 51–75). Austin, TX: University of Texas Press.

CHAPTER 7

Evolving Media Issues: Surveillance and Democracy in the Digital Era

> "One of the effects of living with electric information is that we live habitually in a state of information overload. There's always more than you can cope with"
>
> —*Marshall McLuhan*

A New Era of Democracy?

It has become one of the truisms of the digital era that the rise of so-called interactive media—technologies that allow viewers to respond, to provide information about themselves, and to create their own media content—is a form of democratization. We are told that the Internet will empower consumers and citizens, that more participation means greater control over the media, and that even seemingly trivial forms of "interactive" popular culture like reality TV represent a new era of cultural democratization, in part because "anyone" can become a celebrity. Such accounts tend to equate interactivity with participation and participation with democracy. The result is a rather indiscriminate use of the term "democratization"—one that tends to de-politicize it and to equate it with greater market choice, new forms of commercial customization, and enhanced forms of public participation in consumer culture. A society in which viewers can vote for their favorite contestants on a singing contest may be a more participatory one, but it is not necessarily a more democratic one—at least if the term is to retain any vestige of political meaning.

Such accounts need to be tempered by the recognition that the Pop Idol franchise and its various spinoffs can thrive in authoritarian as well as in democratic societies. Often the forms of so-called participation on offer in the digital era are simply techniques for collecting information about consumers and viewers. These techniques serve as strategies for offloading the work of market research onto consumers by finding ways to induce them to provide more detailed information about themselves, their friends, their behavior and their consumer preferences. This chapter considers the ways in which the equation of new forms of interactivity with participation serves as an alibi for surveillance without necessarily enhancing forms of democratic self-rule.

From *Introduction to Communication Studies: Translating Scholarship into Meaningful Practice* by Alan K. Goodboy and Kara Shultz. Copyright © 2012 by Alan K. Goodboy and Kara Shultz. Reprinted by permission of Kendall Hunt Publishing Company.

Surveillance and Participation in the Digital Economy

If we are to understand democracy as a system in which members of the public participate meaningfully in setting the political goals of their society as well as the means for achieving them, it becomes clear that participation in marketing to ourselves is something altogether different. Increasingly, the interactive economy allows viewers, consumers, and citizens to participate by expressing their preferences and providing feedback, but this is something quite different from democracy, because users do not shape the goals that this information serves: usually increased sales and profits for private entities. Successful reality TV franchises like *Britain's Got Talent* and *Pop Star,* for example, dispense with the need for focus group testing of new artists, since the audience serves as a nationwide, or in some cases, even a region-wide focus group. Interactive web sites that provide "free" services do so in exchange for the ability to collect and use information about consumers. Google provides us with mail and document storage, driving maps, and a search engine in exchange for the ability to capture increasingly detailed information about our behavior and preferences. Facebook gives us a way to stay in touch with our friends and to share pictures with them in exchange for access to detailed information about our social lives and behavior. In both cases, this information is used in ways that are often not transparent to us in order to market to us more effectively. In the digital era, those who have access to the technology are entering a more interactive world, and a more monitored world, but not necessarily a more democratic one.

This observation is not meant to dismiss the potential of interactive media to enhance democracy but rather to emphasize that such media will not necessarily do so of their own accord. If we want a more democratic society, we will have to bend the technology to fit our purposes rather than relying on a misguided faith in the technology to empower the citizenry on its own. Perhaps most importantly, we will have to address the very real asymmetries in power and knowledge that are coming to characterize the so-called information society. For example, businesses and governments will be able to collect and store more information about the behavior of consumers and citizens than ever before, but it will be harder for people to find out exactly what information is collected about them and who has access to it. The easier and more comprehensive data collection becomes as an oft overlooked byproduct of interactivity, the harder it is to keep track of which institutions are gathering what information for which purposes. Is it even possible to specify the entire range of information that smart phone applications or companies like Google and Facebook collect about us when we use their services? At this point, perhaps the most reasonable response is to assume that *everything* we do using interactive devices and services is recorded and stored—at least temporarily. We encounter this fact regularly when we go online and find ads that are related to web sites we may have visited in the past, places or commodities we have mentioned in our emails, or search terms we may have entered online. If you visit a web site devoted to weight loss, for example, expect to find ads for diet products or services inserted in the content of future web sites that you visit, or even alongside your email messages when you check them online.

As more of our personal, professional, and social lives come to rely upon interactive digital platforms from social networking sites to smart phones, we should assume that most of the details of our movements, our interactions, and our purchases are recorded. We should further understand that much of this information can become available to the state and its various monitoring and surveillance apparatuses, which have become increasingly comprehensive and less transparent in the post-9/11 era (Andrejevic, 2007, pp. 161–163)

Viewed from this perspective, the era of enhanced interactivity is not so much one of citizen and consumer empowerment but one characterized by glaring asymmetries in monitoring and surveillance practices. Admittedly, this is just one lens through which to look at the recent development of the information society—there are also new possibilities for commerce, new forms of political and cultural journalism, new forms of sociability and information sharing, and so on. All of these have the potential to contribute to the process of political deliberation, research, and participation. The lens of surveillance is an important one, however, because of the potential impact it has on power relations in contemporary society and also because it tends to be overlooked by more celebratory accounts of new media. We are much more likely to hear about the conveniences of digital media than about their use for monitoring and surveillance. And we are much more likely to hear about the "democratizing" character of the information era than the new and asymmetrical forms of surveillance it enables.

While it is important to acknowledge the very real conveniences and advances associated with the development of digital media technologies, it is also important to address the implications they have for questions of surveillance and power. In return for the many conveniences and advances provided by digital media, we have unthinkingly committed ourselves to the unprecedented privatization of the infrastructure for our social and communicative lives. We tend to treat the companies that populate this infrastructure like Google and Facebook almost as public utilities, entrusting them with the content of our lives and paying for their free services with our personal information.

It is tempting to imagine, at least in media savvy circles, that this exchange is a matter of informed consent—that we understand precisely what we are surrendering in return for access to interactive services—but the fact is, even those few who carefully peruse terms of service agreements and privacy policies have only the vaguest idea of what information is captured about them and how it is used. The policies themselves are general, vague, and subject to ongoing change without notice. Those who own the infrastructure of the digital world we are coming to inhabit set the terms of the exchange and the rest of us are obliged to accept them or go without.

We might describe the migration of our communicative lives onto commercially monitored platforms as a process of digital "enclosure"—one whereby a growing range of activities, transactions, and interactions become encompassed by the monitoring embrace of an interactive (virtual) space (for more on the notion of digital enclosure see Boyle, 2003). Accompanying this movement is a not-so-subtle shift in social relations: not so much the end of privacy, but the privatization and commodification of personal information at an unprecedented level. The process of digital enclosure clearly has a spatial component, insofar as it relies on the expansion of an interactive communication infrastructure that includes broadband and cellular, as well as digital TV and radio. As these networks encompass new spaces, they enter into a monitored, interactive, "virtual" enclosure. These can intersect with and overlap one another. We might, for example, log onto the Internet over morning coffee via smart phone or laptop—thereby generating information about our location, browsing habits, email use, and so on. During the course of the day, we might use GPS systems, cellular networks, and various kinds of "smart" cards to pay tolls, ride mass transit, or shop. All of these interactive systems lend themselves to the generation of cybernetic information: feedback about the transactions and interactions they enable. This feedback becomes the property of private companies that can store, aggregate, sort, and, in many cases, sell the information to others.

The promise of interactivity comes into its own in the realm of politics—the realm from which the popular reception of new media as democratic is drawn. The rhetoric is a familiar one: Now anyone (who has access) can talk back, can have their voice heard, and can create their own media content. Everyone (who has access) has become a publisher, a creator, a participant in our public culture. For example, the claims of new media theorist and game designer Celia Pearce (1997) neatly complement those of ubiquitous political consultant and cyber-celebrant Joe Trippi (2004). Both invoke the promise of technologically facilitated democratic revolution as a natural outcome of digital media. As Pearce puts it, "The digital age introduces a new form of international socialism, a new kind of democracy that Marx never even imagined" (1997, 180). The story of the political deployment of the Internet is, according to Trippi, a story of the revitalization of democracy: "Most of all it's the story of people standing up and making themselves heard. It's the story of how to engage those Americans in a real dialogue, how to reach them where they live, how to stop *selling* to them and start *listening* to them" (2004, XX). This opposition is a misleading one. The emerging model of data-driven relationship marketing undermines the opposition described by Trippi: The sellers are able to sell more effectively precisely because they are able to listen more efficiently.

The real question that needs to be addressed is how new media technologies are being turned to political ends not in theory, but in *practice.* And increasingly this means the use of monitoring and marketing strategies by politicians. It is one thing to say with Joe Trippi that the Internet could be the "most democratizing innovation we've ever seen," (2004, p. 235) and quite another to consider the ways in which it is being used as one of the most powerful technologies for centralized information gathering, sorting, and management that we've ever seen. Political consultants—never far behind the marketers—have realized for some time that market research algorithms can yield information that is useful not just for selling products, but for recruiting voters. The problem was finding cheap and efficient ways to gather and sort the information. One political consultant, for example, recalled how research revealed several decades ago, "that Mercury owners were far more likely to vote Republican than owners of any other kind of automobile—data that was so constant across the country . . . that it couldn't possibly have been the product of chance. 'We never had the money or the technology to make anything of it . . . But of course, they do now'" (Gertner, 2004, B1).

Just as background details like education level, place of residence, and reading habits help predict what types of products a consumer is likely to buy, they can serve as reliable indicators of which hot-button political issues voters care about. At least that's what political consultants are telling parties and candidates. As the former head of the Republican National Committee put it, "We can tailor our message to people who care about taxes, who care about health care, who care about jobs, who care about regulation—we can target that way" (Gertner, 2004, p. B1). The result is a change in the mode of address adopted by political campaigners. Instead of tailoring a general message designed to maximize common appeal and minimize offense, the goal is to target individuals and groups based on key motivating issues. Whereas the prevailing political wisdom had been to avoid districts heavily populated by opposition party voters, target marketing allowed for tactical poaching: "The advantage of data-based targeting is that political field operatives can home in on precisely the voters they wish to reach—the antiabortion parishioners of a traditionally Democratic African American church congregation, for instance" (Edsall, 2006, p. A1).

This "niche-marketing" approach requires the same asymmetry of information in the political as in the commercial realm: the accumulation of detailed information about consumers combined, ideally, with a corresponding *lack* of information about alternatives (or undesirable aspects of the product being pushed) on the part of consumers. As one political consultant put it: "The nightmare scenario is that the databases create puppet masters" (Gertner, 2004, p. B1). In this nightmare vision—the one whose monitoring apparatus is currently being assembled by political consultants and database experts in anticipation of upcoming elections, "every voter will get a tailored message based on detailed information about the voter. The candidate would know what schools the voter went to, any public records that showed they supported some cause, any court case they've been involved in. There might even be several different messages sent by a candidate to the same home—one for the wife, one for the husband and one for the 23-year-old kid" (Gertner, 2004, p. B1).

Far from public empowerment and democratic rebellion, such a scenario envisions what one commentator describes as "a nearly perfect perversion of the political process": "The candidate knows everything about the voter, but the media and the public know nothing about what the candidate really believes" (Gertner, 2004, p. B1).

Like marketers, political data-miners can harness emerging interactive technologies to the ends of political research. Consider, for example, the case of Knowledge Networks, an instant polling company founded by two Stanford political scientists who realized, like market researchers before them, the information-gathering capability of interactive communication technology. Knowledge Networks turned the TiVo model of interactive content delivery into an instant political polling mechanism by spending millions of dollars to equip more than 40,000 homes of selected viewers with Web TVs. The viewers received the interactive TV device—their portal into the digital enclosure—free of cost in exchange for agreeing to spend 10 minutes a week answering pollsters' questions over the Internet (Lewis, 2000, pp. 65 ff.). In addition to the weekly polls, the Web TVs gather detailed information about viewing habits and Web surfing behavior that can be used to create profiles of the respondents. The device that is used to gather instant responses to, for example, the performance of candidates during a political debate, also collects a constant stream of information about viewers even when they aren't directly engaged in the polling process.

One of the reasons for the increasing value of information captured within the embrace of the digital enclosure is that it does double- and triple-duty: for marketing, policing, and campaigning, By embracing sites of domesticity, leisure, and labor, and permitting always-on connectivity, the interactive digital enclosure provides information not just in discrete packets—a survey here, a focus-group there—but a continuous flow of data.

In a world in which digital media are used to create better informed citizens and to provide them with the means for engaging in public deliberation, for expressing themselves, and for holding their elected officials accountable, the Internet may well enhance democracy. However, in a world in which interactive media are used to monitor citizens and consumers more thoroughly in order to market to them more effectively, there is no guarantee that the ability to interact strengthens modern democracies. The world imagined by marketers and political consultants is all too often one in which interactive technology can be used to perfect strategies for target marketing and the centralized management of public opinion by political elites.

Possible Futures

At stake in these alternative versions of the future—one of empowerment, the other of centralized control—is the very meaning of the term "democratic participation." By participation, do we simply mean the ability to provide increasingly detailed information about ourselves? If so, then the offer of participation can double as an alibi for the perfection of marketing strategies—both political and commercial. If, however, by participation, we mean a conscious, considered, informed, and meaningful contribution to the governing process, it is important to distinguish this at every turn from a version of participation that equates submission to detailed monitoring with participation. Democratic politics promises public participation all the way up, as it were, to the goal-setting process itself. A second element of democracy—one emphasized by constitutional scholar Cass Sunstein (2002)—is the creation of optimal conditions for public deliberation *about* shared goals. As Sunstein suggests, the adoption of marketing and advertising techniques by political campaigns ignores an important difference between consumer decisions and political decisions. The former relate to individual preferences and only indirectly influence society as a whole, whereas the latter are explicitly about collective decisions that (directly) influence society as a whole. My decision to buy a particular laundry detergent does not have broader social consequences in quite the same way as does my vote for a new school tax proposal or a Congressional candidate. Moreover, as Sunstein argues, political participation envisions a decision-making process that "does not take individual tastes as fixed or given. It prizes democratic self-government, understood as a requirement of 'government by discussion,' accompanied by reason-giving in the public domain" (Sunstein, 2002, p. 37).

The database-informed customized campaign model of political marketing transposes the perfection of what Sunstein might describe as a consumerist model onto the political process. Far from contributing to democratic participation and deliberation, the version of interactivity envisioned by the database consultants and target marketers offers to perfect a cybernetic form of public relations: the customization of marketing appeals based on detailed profiles of individual voters. The consequences of this model of interactivity are threefold: the further disaggregation of the citizenry, the facilitation of sorting and exclusion when it comes to information access, and the further normalization of surveillance as a legitimate political tool.

Database politics transforms government publicity into target marketing and citizen publicity into increasingly precise market research. It equates submission to detailed forms of monitoring with democratic participation—and feedback with shared control. In so doing, it reduces what Sunstein calls citizen sovereignty—the collective expression of shared political concerns arrived at through public deliberation—to what he calls consumer sovereignty—the "individualized" preferences of the shopper. In so doing, it further enables the importation of marketing and public relations strategies into the political process. The goal of these strategies is not to become increasingly responsible to the public will, but to find ways of managing it more effectively before it expresses itself in action. As media theorist Jodi Dean observes, "Perhaps paradoxically, the very means of democratic publicity end up leading to its opposite: private control by the market" (Dean, 2002, p. 150). Avoiding this outcome depends on our will to distinguish between meaningful participation and the process of providing marketers with more information about ourselves. It will depend on developing media technologies that serve the interests of citizens in addition to those of consumers.

References

Andrejevic, M. (2007). *iSpy: surveillance and power in the interactive era.* Lawrence, KS: University of Kansas Press.

Boyle, J. (2003). The second enclosure movement and the construction of the public domain. *Law and Contemporary Problems, 66,* 147–178.

Dean, J. (2002). *Publicity's secret: How technoculture capitalizes on democracy.* Ithaca: Cornell University Press.

Edsall, T. (2006). Democrats' data mining stirs an intraparty battle. *The Washington Post,* March 8, A1.

Gertner, J. (2004). The very, very personal is political. *The New York Times Magazine,* 15 February, B1.

Lewis, M. (2000). The two-bucks-a-minute democracy. *The New York Times Magazine,* 5 November, 65–72.

Pearce, C. (1997). *The interactive book.* New York: Penguin.

Sunstein, C. (2002). *Republic.com.* Princeton, NJ: Princeton University Press.

Trippi, J. (2004). *The revolution will not be televised.* NY: ReganBooks.

SECTION 3
Exploring Cultural Studies

CHAPTER 8

Understanding Cultural Studies

> "Yesterday's deconstructions are often tomorrow's orthodox clichés."
>
> —*Stuart Hall*

A quick look at most texts discussing what cultural studies "is" can be a distressing experience for the undergraduate student. Often, less space is devoted to what it *is* as is given to what it *is not*. Additionally, the student will often confront competing constructions of what it *does* in relation to what it does *not do*. A quick Google search can add to the confusion, as there are innumerable pages devoted to the term "cultural studies".

Miller asserts that cultural studies is "a tendency across disciplines, rather than a discipline itself. This is evident in practioners simultaneously expressed desires to: refuse definition, insist on differentiation, and sustain conventional departmental credentials" (Miller, 2006, p. 1). The first somewhat dim picture of cultural studies that begins to emerge from such a representation is slightly maddening: it resists being defined means this will not be a simple undertaking. What further complicates the issue is that if cultural studies is viewed—as Miller suggests—as a "tendency" rather than as a discipline, what should we make by the a list of graduate and undergraduate programs in cultural studies that another quick Google search will uncover? The student just wading into this arena might take some comfort by these programs' use of the term interdisciplinary to explain their sites of academic investigation.

Indeed, the complexity surrounding the question "what is cultural studies" has been thoughtfully analyzed by researchers such as Chris Barker in his text *Cultural Studies: Theory and Practice* (2000, 2011). Usefully, he tells us that the "cultural" in cultural studies is different from the study of culture, which takes places in departments such as anthropology and sociology[1].

For Stuart Hall (often called one of the founding fathers of cultural studies and whom we will meet shortly), Barker reminds us, "what is at stake is the connection that cultural studies seeks to make to matters of power and cultural politics. That is, to an exploration of representations of and 'for' marginalized social groups and the need for cultural change" (Barker, 2011, p. 5).

---

[1] Of course we can—and often do—find practioners of cultural studies in these areas as well. Barker is referring to the more traditional study of culture (with, ultimately, various definitions of culture).

Indeed during the mid-twentieth century, the linkage of the concept of power to the cultural domain was a site of investigation taken up by the intellectuals of the Frankfurt School using what they termed critical theory, and which was broadly influenced by reinterpretations of Marxism. It is instructive, therefore, to briefly examine some of their ideas, as well as those of the Italian communist Antonio Gramsci, whose works very much influenced Stuart Hall and other British "founding fathers" of cultural studies. By sketching the influences on cultural studies in twentieth-century history, we can come to a better understanding of its various conceptions today.

Critical Theory and the Frankfurt School

The early part of the twentieth century saw the growth of intellectual engagement with media culture. In 1923, a wealthy young German Marxist, Felix Weil, provided funding to form the Institute for Social Research (commonly referred to as the Frankfurt School), founded specifically to bring together different schools of Marxist thought and to advance new research within a neo-Marxist framework. In 1930, Max Horkheimer, also given a chair in Social Philosophy at the University of Frankfurt, became director of the institute. He championed interdisciplinary research within social theory, which was exemplified by his helping to usher in a heavier focus on psychoanalysis (Wolfreys, 2006a).

Among the group of mostly Jewish intellectuals that formed the Frankfurt School were Theodor W. Adorno, Leo Lowenthal, Herbert Marcuse, Eric Fromm and Walter Benjamin. Most of these intellectuals would relocate after the Nazi ascension to power; by 1935, the School had found itself in the US[2].

A new critical theory emerged within the Frankfurt School both in Germany and during its period in exile; its application to the media is of interest to us here. In their book *Dialectic of Enlightenment* (1947), one of the most important publications of the Frankfurt School, Horkheimer and Adorno coined the term *culture industry*. What did they mean by this? Referring to an earlier, 1944 version of this book's manuscript, Adorno specified that: "In our drafts, we spoke of 'mass culture'. We replaced that expression with 'culture industry' in order to exclude from the outset the interpretation agreeable to its advocates: that it is a matter of something like a culture that arises spontaneously from the masses themselves, the contemporary form of popular art. From the latter the culture industry must be distinguished in the extreme" (Adorno, 2009, p. 15). Douglas Kellner says Adorno and Horkheimer used this term to:

> signify the process of the industrialization of mass-produced culture and the commercial imperatives that drove the system. The critical theorists analyzed all mass-mediated cultural artifacts within the context of industrial production, in which the commodities of the culture industries exhibited the same features as other products of mass production: commodification, standardization, and massification. The culture industries had the specific function, however, of providing ideological legitimation of the existing capitalist societies and of integrating individuals into its way of life (Kellner, 2014).

From this perspective (one which many cultural studies scholars today negate), the masses were not active producers of their own culture; instead, they were its passive and uncritical consumers, gobbling up without question the cultural products, artifacts, and ideas sold—or presented—to them. Adorno

---

[2] Adorno would reluctantly move to the US in 1938, but Walter Benjamin, for a variety of reasons, never made it across the ocean. Instead, he moved to France. In 1940, Horkheimer managed to secure a visa to the US for Benjamin, who believing he would not make it (and already known to be suffering from depression), committed suicide on the Franco-Spanish border with the visa still in his pocket.

and Horkheimer believed the goods produced by the culture industry had exactly the opposite effect of what "high art" should achieve—to develop critically conscious and politically engaged consumers.

Unlike traditional Marxism, which focused on economy, Adorno and Horkheimer saw culture as the root of apathy; remember they were writing as refugees of the murderous Nazi regime and as such in the US—a place engulfed by popular culture and its shallow entertainments. In other words, culture as an industry maintained the status quo; people did not question the dominant ideology, which supported the needs of the elite (producers) at the expense of the consuming masses. This, Adorno and Horkheimer pessimistically noted, was happening in an era of tremendous achievements in technology, in the sciences, in industry, in medicine, and the culture industry nurtured this apathy among the average consumers.

The Frankfurt School's main contribution was to analyze media and media industries within a Marxist framework. A larger influence on cultural studies as it emerged in the UK was the writings of Antonio Gramsci, one of the founders of the Communist Party of Italy (CPI) in 1921. As Morton succinctly states, "In the 50 years since Gramsci first became an 'object' of study, his theories and concepts have left their mark on virtually every field in the humanities and the social sciences. His writings have been interpreted, appropriated, and even instrumentalised in many different and often conflicting ways" (Morton, 2007, p. ix).

Antonio Gramsci and *The Prison Notebooks*

Gramsci, born on the Italian island of Sardinia in 1891, became head of the CPI in 1924, when he was also elected into the Italian Chamber of Deputies (similar to the American senate). However, it is of little surprise that the far-right Fascist legislature of the time would shortly arrest and try their political rivals, Gramsci included. Indeed, at Gramsci's trial, the prosecutor would ominously state: "We must prevent this brain from functioning for 20 years" (Gramsci & Henderson, 1988, p. 7).

Although he would spend almost the rest of his short life in prison (he was released on medical grounds before he died in 1937), the Fascist government could not in the least prevent Gramsci's brain from "functioning"; on the contrary, it was from within Mussolini's jails that Gramsci wrote his essays on culture, Fascism, communism, and power that would be published as *The Prison Notebooks* years later, and rather unfortunately, only translated to English in 1971.

For our purposes, Gramsci's enduring legacy has been his conceptualization of *cultural hegemony*, which rearticulated Marx's use of the term *ideology*. In *The German Ideology*, Marx wrote: "The ideas of the ruling class are in every epoch the ruling ideas … The class which has the means of material production at its disposal, has control over the means of mental production at its disposal, so that thereby, generally speaking, the ideas of those who lack the means of mental production are subject to it" (Marx, 1996, p. 186). In other words, ideology is the worldview or perspectives of those who are in power, as they control the tools (media, for our purposes) which disseminate ideas of a culture. This in turn shapes the perspective of the rest of society.

Ideological positions are accordingly functions of economics. Do the interests of the ruling class mirror those of the rest, the working classes? From this perspective, it does not matter as even if the dominant ideology is in fact directly opposite to the interests of the working classes, the latter hold up and emulate the dominant ideology as their own; Marx termed this condition as "false consciousness" (Wolfreys, 2006, p. 139). A good example might be to think of the beauty industry. By marketing a certain idea of beauty (say thinness), the advertising industry supports and disseminates the idea of what beautiful is. Accepting such conceptions, the rest of us spend billions to consume products/services designed to help us meet that ideal and feel good about ourselves.

In the process the producers/owners of the goods we buy are enriched as we struggle to meet the standards of beauty they have defined for us and disseminated amongst us.

Gramsci's concept of hegemony draws on ideology as articulated by Marx, but it looks beyond economics and politics to explicate how the powerful (as suggested in the quote above) subject the rest to their ways of thinking. From Gramsci's perspective, the ruling classes' worldview is cemented *with* the consensus of the working classes; the dominant ideology is presented as the natural way of things, or as common sense, as Gramsci termed it. Force is not necessary for the dominant ideology to be accepted; instead, the ruling classes use various modes of persuasion to make it seem natural to all, as for "power to be durable, it must also be persuasive, educative and work to promote a consensus typified by the acceptance of a common sense" (Wolfreys, 2006, p. 138). So the idea that thin is beautiful seems normal to us—we do not usually question why that is so. Gramsci used the term hegemony to describe how the ruling classes are able to present their worldview in a way that becomes normal and common sense for the rest of us.

Gramsci also notes that there are shifting allegiances and alliances between social classes, so in this sense there is not one dominant class. On the one hand, the ruling class tries to create consensus in ways that protect its own interests. On the other hand, the various subordinate classes try to create a space for their own worldview and their own needs. This complicates matters, while the powerful do their best to have their ideas transmitted and accepted by all, at the same time the subordinate classes (the rest of us) also struggle to have our definitions and worldview validated. Thus culture is a contested site, and hegemony requires compromise (Goldberg, 2011).

Although some have pointed to the inconsistent way in which Gramsci used the term hegemony (and who can wonder, writing as he did from a Fascist jail), this term, with its meaning appropriated and applied differently, would become foundational to cultural studies, especially as articulated by the various New Left academics in 1960's Great Britain.

Beginnings: The New Left in Britain

In his autobiography *Interesting Times* (2002), the British Marxist historian Eric Hobsbawm (1917–2012) describes how the rise of Fascism in pre-WW2 Europe led many individuals across the European continent to join Stalinist movements or parties.

However, in the postwar era, and at the height of the cold war, at least two global events in 1956 would give rise to the British New Left—a movement of intellectuals and students who would break with what we might term as the Old Left, the communist and communist-leaning groups whose views and politics remained fairly static. For our purposes of introducing cultural studies, notable figures among the New Left (whose works are necessary reading for those delving into cultural studies) were E. P. Thompson, who published *The Making of the English Working Class* in 1963[3], Richard Hoggart, Stuart Hall (more about them below), and Raymond Williams, whose intellectual curiosity and contributions were beautifully summarized by Stuart Hall in *The New Statesman*.

The Life of Raymond Williams

http://www.newstatesman.com/society/2008/02/work-life-williams-english

---

[3] To learn more about Thompson and his writings there is a very good collection of some of his hard-to-find essays. Winslow, Calvin, Thompson, E. P. *E. P. Thompson and the Making of the New Left: Essays and Polemics*. London: Lawrence & Wishart Ltd, 2014.

The first global event repudiated by the New Left was the brutal suppression of the Hungarian uprising by the Soviet Union in 1956. The second was the invasion of the Suez Canal by British and French forces.

It is instructive to produce in some length what Stuart Hall has written about the New Left's genesis:

> The 'first' New Left was born in 1956, a conjuncture—not just a year—bounded on one side by the suppression of the Hungarian Revolution by Soviet tanks and on the other by the British and French invasion of the Suez Canal zone. These two events, whose dramatic impact was heightened by the fact that they occurred within days of each other, unmasked the underlying violence and aggression latent in the two systems that dominated political life at the time—Western imperialism and Stalinism—and sent a shock wave through the political world. … 'Suez' underlined the enormity of the error in believing that lowering the Union Jack in a few excolonies necessarily signalled the 'end of imperialism', or that the real gains of the welfare state and the widening of material affluence meant the end of inequality and exploitation. 'Hungary' and 'Suez' were thus liminal, boundary-marking experiences. They symbolized the break-up of the political Ice Age (Hall, 2010, p. 177).

The New Left came into existence in the aftermath of these two events. It attempted to define a third political space somewhere between these two metaphors. Its rise signified for people on the left in my generation the end of the imposed silences and political impasses of the Cold War, and the possibility of a breakthrough into a new socialist project (Hall, 2010).

The New Left intellectuals were accordingly vocal in their rejection colonialism (at this time, while some countries such as India had gained political independence, many others across the globe were still part of the British Empire), dismayed by how that independence could be blithely toyed with by former colonialists (as the invasion of Egypt's Suez by the British and French made clear), and finally, disenchanted by the cold-war politics which did little to improve people's lives.

Hungarian uprising

http://www. historylearningsite. co.uk/hungarian_ uprising_1956.htm

The Suez Crisis

https://history.state.gov/ milestones/1953–1960/ suez

Birmingham Centre for Contemporary Cultural Studies

What is known as British cultural studies emerged from intellectuals deeply associated with the New Left of the late 1950s, particularly the four individuals already mentioned: Richard Hoggart, Raymond Williams, E. P. Thompson and Stuart Hall. It is instructive to note Hoggart and Williams grew up in poor working-class families at a time when the expectation was that young men would quite school and help support the family. They instead both went to university and would teach adult education—something Stuart Hall was also engaged in. These teaching experiences deeply influenced their work in cultural studies (Laing, 1991).

By the 1960s, Great Britain faced dramatic changes, some of which rocked its traditional (read white, upper class) conceptions of self. Its colonies across the globe were fighting for—and claiming—political independence, challenging and collapsing self-conceptions of empire. There was a tremendous inflow of people from South Asia and the Caribbean, challenging conceptions of white identity and "Britishness". The tremendous explosion of modern mass communication, especially television, and the flux of American culture would further contribute to this erosion of traditional British identity.

Hoggart, 1918–2014
· · · · · · · · · · · · · ·

http://www.
theguardian.com/
books/2014/apr/10/
richard-hoggart

Richard Hoggart was particularly focused on assessing mass communication, specifically how the popular magazines and newspapers of the day affected the values of the working classes. This concern was at the root of Hoggart's seminal book *Uses of Literacy* (1958), without which, Stuart Hall has argued, "there would have been no Cultural Studies" (Hall, 2007, p. 40). Hoggart suggested that the working classes were not simply blank slates onto which the mass media (controlled as they were by the powerful elites) could simply imprint the ideas they wanted the masses to follow. Rather, Hoggart argued, the working classes had their own lived culture, and media might at best actively negotiate meanings with their already-existing culture (Hall, 2007).

In 1964, two years after he became a professor of English, Hoggart helped found the Centre for Contemporary Cultural Studies (CCCS) at the University of Birmingham to study mass culture, and he invited Stuart Hall, who had helped found the *New Left Review* journal in 1960, to join him. From the start, their focus was on collaborative research across disciplines; cultural studies, was from its inception, interdisciplinary.

Stuart Hall was born into a mixed-race family in a Jamaica still under British rule. The racial politics (his parents feared he was too dark to succeed on the island) led him to Oxford University as a 19-year-old Rhodes scholar in 1951. He has said of that experience: "I realized the moment I got to Oxford was that someone like me could not really be part of it … I mean, I could make a success there, I could even be perhaps accepted into it, but I would never feel it was my place. It's the summit of something else. It's distilled Englishness" (Yardely, 2014).

Rather than completing his PhD dissertation, Hall immersed himself in the New Left, and by 1964, had, as mentioned, joined Hoggart at the newly formed CCCS. Hall would become its director four years or so later and hold that position until 1979, by which time the innovative research and approaches to culture undertaken at the CCCS would have a profound impact on academic inquiry around the world.

Hall and other researchers collaborating at the CCCS theorized about media differently than usual (see earlier chapters). They moved away from the stimulus-response models (you see/read something, you react accordingly). They examined culture industries as theorized by the Frankfurt School but drew different assumptions and conclusions as they enriched their work using and reframing Gramsci's conceptualization of hegemony (in particular the idea that meanings and culture are negotiated). They borrowed from (and published) works on semiotics[4]—the study of

---

[4] The Swiss linguist Ferdinand de Saussure (1857–1913) coined the term semiology (semiotics). Around the same time the American philosopher Charles Sanders Peirce (1839–1914) developed a theory on signs and their interpretation. De Saussure's work would influence an array of mid-century intellectuals such as the anthropologist Claude Lévi-Strauss (1908–2009), the philosophers Louis Althusser (1918–1990) and Michel Foucault (1926–1984), and the literary critic/semiotician Roland Barthes (1915–1980), to name just a few whose works would leave a mark on cultural studies.

signs—to assess how messages are interpreted. They rejected the idea of a mass audience, arguing instead that an audience is made up of very different types of people, and thus the way individuals decode messages would be based on various factors that may (or may not) accord with what the powerful media elite wanted to express. Among the very far-reaching consequences was that cultural studies became a very firmly entrenched approach across disciplines at universities across the globe[5].

And So?

Today one finds numerous papers studying mass culture and people's lived experiences within a cultural-studies perspective. Researchers analyze texts (the written word, films, images, symbols) using a variety of research tools—textual analysis, ethnographic fieldwork, and so forth.

The study of popular culture has gained currency; the study of ethnicity, race and gender has become normal. We talk of intertextuality to explore the intersections of various themes, approaches and texts. Papers exploring pop-cultural icons such as Beyoncé, Britney Spears, J-Lo, and artists such as Banksy abound. News production research, particularly in the US, continues to examine the manufacturing of information by media conglomerates and the manner news/information is normalized for audiences. University courses have been taught about Jay-Z. These studies exist across disciplines (communication and media studies, feminist and gender studies, ethnic studies, English, languages, etc.) and within specifically designated cultural studies and popular culture departments and programs.

In short, the cultural studies provides an open-ended framework by which to examine—and to theorize—about social life. It remains a contested site that still engenders tremendous debate, as can be seen in the exchanges about its relevance and its directions that took place just a few years ago.

Michael Bérubé: What's the Matter with Cultural Studies?

http://chronicle.com/ article/Whats-the-Matter-With/48334/

Responding to Bérubé

https://bullybloggers. wordpress.com/ 2009/09/23/a-note-from-the-unicorns/

---

[5] This focus on the Birmingham school is important as a starting point. However, it is instructive to note as Hoggart was setting up the CCCS, business was not going on as usual in the rest of the world. In the US, the 1960s were characterized by massive upheavals, and its New Left communist/socialist groups were very much involved in antiracist movements and consequently had large membership among the young African-American militant movements. Leftist students and intellectuals in South America were framing their struggles against established military dictatorships. In the newly politically-independent countries—and others at the cusp of independence—of Asia and Africa, anticold war sentiments had led to the non-aligned movement, which rejected colonialism, neo-colonialism, and the pressures exerted by the more powerful nations of the cold war. In universities across the world, then, new approaches to the study of society were emerging in tandem.

Stuart Hall, in discussing the theoretical legacies of cultural studies, once said that theory might be viewed as a "set of contested, localized, conjunctural knowledges, which have to be debated in a dialogical way. But also as a practice which always thinks about its intervention in a world in which it would make some difference, in which it would have some effect" (Hall, 1996, p. 286).

References

Adorno, T. W. (2009). "Culture industry reconsidered" in *Media Studies*: A Reader in T. Sue, B. Caroline, & M. Paul (Eds.), *A reader* (3rd ed., p. 15). New York, NY: New York University Press.

Barker, C. (2011). *Cultural studies: Theory and practice* (3rd ed). Thousand Oaks, CA: SAGE.

Goldberg, M. L. (2014). Retrieved from https://faculty.washington.edu/mlg/courses/definitions/hegemony.html

Gramsci, A., & Hamish. H. (1998). *Gramsci's prison letters: A selection*. London: Zwan Publications. [*eBook Academic Collection (EBSCOhost)*, EBSCOhost (accessed October 23, 2014) p. 7]

Hall, S. (1996). Cultural studies and its theoretical legacies. In D. Morley & K-. H. Chen (Eds.), *Critical dialogues in cultural studies*. London: Routledge, pp. 277–294.

Hall S. (2007). Richard Hoggart, The uses of literacy and the cultural turn. *International Journal of Cultural Studies*, 10(1), 39–49.

Hall, S. (2010). Life and times of the first "New Left." *New Left Review, 62*, 177–196.

Kellner, D. (2014). The Frankfurt School. Retrieved from http://pages.gseis.ucla.edu/faculty/kellner/essays/frankfurtschool2.pdf

Laing, S. (1991). Raymond Williams and the cultural analysis of television. *Media, Culture and Society, 13*, 153–169.

Marx, K. (1996). The German ideology. In J. Appelby, E. Covington, & D. Hoyt (Eds.), *Knowledge and postmodernism in historical perspective*. New York: Routledge.

Miller, T. (2006). *A companion to cultural studies*. Malden, MA: Blackwell Publishing.

Morton, A. D. (2007). *Unravelling Gramsci: Hegemony and passive revolution in the global political economy*. London: Pluto Press. Retrieved from http://site.ebrary.com/id/10480197

Wolfreys, J. (2006a). *Modern European criticism and theory: A critical guide*. Edinburgh: Edinburgh University Press.

Yardley, W. (2014). Trailblazing British scholar of multicultural influences, is dead at 82. *New York Times*. Retrieved from http://www.nytimes.com/2014/02/18/world/europe/stuart-hall-trailblazing-british-scholar-of-multicultural-influences-is-dead-at-82.html?r=0

CHAPTER 9

Cultural Studies: Representation, Relations of Power and the Self

> "A society is not fully available for analysis until each of its practices
> is included"
>
> —*Raymond Williams*

Season 5 of the UK reality television show *Celebrity Big Brother* was both its highest rated season and its most controversial. The scandal of the season involved the racist verbal abuse of housemate and famed Bollywood star Shilpa Shetty by housemates Danielle Lloyd (model), reality TV star Jade Goody, her boyfriend Jack Tweed, Goody's mother Jackiey Budden, and singer Jo O'Meara. Instances of abuse included: Budden referring to Shetty as "the Indian" rather than using her name, Tweed making monkey noises while calling her a "f******g c***," Lloyd commanding Shetty to "f*** off home . . . [because] she can't even speak English properly," and Goody attacking Shetty's authenticity and class status by telling her to go live in a "slum," while also referring to her as "Shilpa poppadum" (Singh, 2007; Revoir, 2007; Blake, 2007; Bashir, 2007).

London's mayor, Ken Livingston, criticized broadcaster Channel 4 for pandering to racism by selecting and airing such racist clips, simply in order to gain a larger audience and more advertisers (Blake, 2007). Viewers responded to Shetty's treatment on the show by filing nearly 50,000 complaints during the month-long season with Britain's television regulator, the Office of Communication (Ofcom). Ultimately, Ofcom found Channel 4 breached the broadcasting code by making "serious editorial misjudgements (sic)." As a result, Channel 4 was required to apologize on air and broadcast unedited transcripts of the even more racist unaired moments (Conlan, 2007). Advertisers responded by pulling their ads and sponsorships.

The already infamous season 5 also touched off an international media melee when Indians burned an effigy of the producers of the show during then Minister of Finance Gordon Brown's visit to India. Prime Minister Tony Blair made a statement in an attempt to salvage Britain's reputation after Shetty's treatment on the show became international news. The *Celebrity Big Brother* scandal was revealing, because it showcased not just the racism of the contestants on the show, but correspondingly (through the evolving information about the editing and broadcasting of select clips) the

From *Introduction to Communication Studies: Translating Scholarship into Meaningful Practice* by Alan K. Goodboy and Kara Shultz. Copyright © 2012 by Alan K. Goodboy and Kara Shultz. Reprinted by permission of Kendall Hunt Publishing Company.

producers and editors as well, who chose to air many of the filmed segments, implying their tacit approval of Shetty's verbal harassment by bullies.

This essay takes a critical cultural studies approach to addressing the question: *How do representations of cultural others in popular media shape our understanding of ourselves and our place in society?* In an attempt to answer this question, we do not conduct audience, spectatorship, or reader response analysis to determine precisely how, intellectually, physiologically, or psychologically, representations of cultural others in popular media affect our bodies and our psyches. Nor do we distribute and analyze survey questionnaires or conduct laboratory observations of how images of cultural others shape self-understandings of people and their social positions in the world. Rather, we draw on critical cultural research to theorize the relationship between such representations of cultural others in order to address the notion of selves and of positionality. By *critical cultural,* we mean an approach that addresses relations of power, power situated in multiple ways and that ranges from class to race to mobility, for instance, and that forges new theoretical and methodological vistas in the process by borrowing and re-conceiving disciplinary modalities (see Ono, 2009a; Ono, 2011). We also have *praxis* in mind, how knowledge of this can shape our actions and the world around us. Stuart Hall has addressed this very question in his work on representation, both in a lecture captured in video form, *Stuart Hall: Representation and the Media* (Jhally, 1997), as well as in his book, *The Work of Representation* (1997). Hence, we are indebted to him for many of our insights about this subject, even as we work to build upon his work in order to answer the question posed above.

Hall begins by explaining that each of us has our own "conceptual map," or "maps of meaning," or "frameworks of intelligibility," which Hall uses as synonyms. By these terms, he is suggesting that people see the world through memories of the experiences they have had. That is, people only remember certain things, and they largely remember things they have experienced; hence, one's own unique combination of overlapping experiences leads an individual to having the particular conceptual map she does. As he says in the video,

> Now it could be the case that the conceptual map which I carry around my head is totally different from yours, in which case you and I would interpret or make sense of the world in totally different ways. We would be incapable of sharing our thoughts or expressing ideas about the world to each other. In fact, each of us probably does understand and interpret the world in a unique and individual way (p. 19).

What Hall suggests is that what we remember remains internal to us unless we voice it, tell others, and make it public, what he calls "externalization." Thus, we have memories of what happened to us—our experiences—but only those memories that we vocalize or share in some other way become publicly accessible and available for public consumption, discussion, and comparison to others' conceptual maps.

Historically, representations of people of color were controlled by dominant media industries that were overseen and operated almost exclusively by members of the dominant white racial elite, at least until the civil rights era of the 1950s, the 1960s, and the 1970s (the vast majority still are, by the way) (Noam, 2009). Because those white men did not necessarily know a lot of people of color intimately, hang around people of color, or live in their neighborhoods, for instance, the externalizations put out there by the media did not directly correspond in any real or useful way to the actual lived experiences of people of color. Those externalizations, which emerged out of the experiences of those who made those images, were, therefore, stereotypes, representations that were produced and circulated that came, not from people of color on the ground, but from those with little real knowledge, access, or lived relationship with people of color. Furthermore, those images that some people have called "false" ones were quoted or cited by other media; hence, a well of such images existed as a kind of archive of imagery of people of color that had little to do with their lived realities and experiences (hooks, 1992; Ono, 2009b, 2010; Hall, 2003; Collins, 2000). Those images were odd, indeed, as those representations were neither created by those being represented, nor by people who knew people of color well, which explains how such sometimes bizarre images became the reigning stereotypes of our media culture.

One might argue that, at least during the time period when the vast majority of media images of people of color were not their own externalizations, if one were to see, and hence consume, images of people of color, one was forced to consume images that were not self-made ones, but ones made by others, whose ideas of people of color were neither well informed nor often complimentary.

Many have written that when one does not see images of people like oneself, when one does not see images of people like oneself that are heroes and leads, and when one does not see images of people like oneself that are kind, sensitive, complimentary, and complex, it is possible to have a distorted sense of one's own social position within society and one's social position and worth, as well as one's meaningfulness within society (Dixon & Linz, 2000; Gross, 2001; Ting-Toomey, 2005; Tang, 2007; Morgan, Shanahan & Signorielli, 2009; Martins & Harrison, 2011). Not seeing one's image represented on screen, or seeing one's image in a way that is alienating—hence is quite detached from one's own experience of self-identity—can be psychologically traumatizing. But, seeing problematic representations of people of color also affects those who are not members of the group being represented, including members of the racially dominant society.

So, for members of the dominant culture, images that reinforce problematic images of minority groups means living in a vacuum and operating in a world that is not real. It is fantasy, and it can lead to assumptions, beliefs, decisions, and whole ways of being based on those images that not only are not self-serving, but that may ultimately be socially troubling, as well as ultimately self-defeating. Kent Ono and Vincent Pham (2009) have suggested this in their discussion of yellowface, a practice not unlike blackface, where non Asian Americans played Asian Americans in the theatre, in films, and on television:

> Yellowface also serves a psychosocial function, mediating both the psychological perception of Asians and Asian Americans and the social interaction with them. It allows audiences to think the masquerading actor is both like and not like an Asian or Asian American. Like blackface, yellowface is a form of racial masquerade, a masquerade in which the audience knows the actor is masquerading, that they are not actually Asian (p. 47).

They go on to say:

> Yellowface has a social dimension as well, for it was originally created for the pleasure of white audiences. Hence, it has more to do with the way white people relate to each other than it does with a genuine, humane relationship with Asians and Asian Americans. As Tchen suggests, 'The visual language of yellowface came to signify a universe of meanings having far more to do with the host culture than with who and what were originally being represented' (1999, p. 129.) . . . Tchen says, 'Viewers who believed these representations became imprisoned in a world of racial caricatures and power relations" (Ibid).

Essentially, then, images from the past that continue into the present that were part of historical subjugation and of social separation and stratified racial and classed subservience, and that may continue to do so, facilitate the ability for divisions to exist between the superordinate and subordinate group and group members, thereby having the effect of producing and reproducing, structurally, social positions and locations. It is the case that media are rarely discussed in relationship with structural racism, but part of what we argue here in this essay is in fact that media representations of minority group members are in fact absolutely basic to any theory of institutional and structural racism.

To clarify some of what we have argued, we briefly take up the specific case of mixed race people here. Currently, discourses of a "new" multiracial identity are being circulated in hopes of more easily negotiating those divisions between superordinate and subordinate groups as mixed race people act as a bridge between races. In this way, multiracial people function as a barometer of sorts for the state of race relations, whereas, historically, mixed race people have been represented as the "ultimate race problem." Now, they are proffered both as the solution to the race problem and as the impetus for the (illusory) declining significance of race (Squires, 2007, p. 2). The changes in racial categorization schema in the 2000 Census has given multiracial people political legitimation; now, they are using mass media for cultural legitimation. Squires (2007) makes note of this fact as she reconciles multiracial visibility with the current media landscape:

Multiracial-identified people have built up an impressive set of texts, theories, organizations, and political projects aimed at reconceptualizing mixed race identity, interracial family life, interracial adoption, and state-sanctioned racial terminology to combat and debunk racist myths and practices that oppress multiracial people. Mass media have been important arenas for this project of redefinition. Through publications targeted at multiracial families and individuals, Web sites, best-selling autobiographies, talk show interviews, press conferences, public testimony at government hearings, and 'outing' of multiracial celebrities, multiracial people have used media to disseminate new images and descriptions of their identities and experiences (Squires, 2007 p. 10).

Multiracial exceptionalism, or the hope that multiracial people will transcend race and heal racial divisions, is not the answer to how popular media can better represent cultural others. Having progressed from enduring tropes that rendered mixed race people either invisible, tragic, hybrid degenerates, or the quintessential basis of the "race problem," the current representations of multiracial people do, minimally, demonstrate the power of visibility. Their popularity currently also demonstrates the unequal operation of power, especially when comparing how rapidly mixed race people as a group have increased their visibility within media, and how other groups are still dealing with negative representations and continued marginalization by both media and society.

Representations of cultural others in media are an important source of information through which both dominant and subordinate groups construct their identities, attitudes, and beliefs. However, as a source of information, a number of factors, including media ownership, and enduring historical (mis)representations of others, have resulted in selective depictions that, when existing, are mostly negative or inaccurate and are rarely nuanced or complex. Included in these misrepresentations are instances when people of color offer their own representations, positive and negative, because those representations are still part of a media system in which they have little control. A steady stream of these images (or lack thereof), have been detrimental to the psychosocial development of members of those groups, distorting one's sense of worth and sense of belonging, and reinforcing the idea that the political and cultural exclusion of many marginalized groups is warranted. The higher visibility of mixed race people, rather than being heralded as the solution to the race problem, should be taken as one group's quest to challenge the legacy of the under/mis-representation of cultural others in media and culture. Their emergence has challenged their previously static depictions, and they have been able to shift the meanings attached to historically derogatory images. Recognizing mixed race success cautiously in this realm means also recognizing the privilege mixed race people have been afforded, especially considering that other groups similarly have been attempting to shift representations and meanings attached to their images. However, as groups continue to challenge their characterizations in media and work toward dismantling racial hierarchies by creating connections in contrast to media produced divisions between groups, new social realities may be created for media to model. And, new, more productive identities may be forged.

References

Bashir, M., (Anchor) & Wright, D. (Reporter). (2007). Bigot brother? Reality racism. [Television], *Nightline*: ABC.

Blake, J. (Reporter). (2007). Bigot Brother? [Television], *CNN News.*

Browne, A., O'Connor, A., Webster, P., & Sherwin, A. (2007, January 18). Reality TV creates a very surreal diplomatic crisis, *The Times (London).*

Collins, P. H. (2000). Mammies, matriarchs, and other controlling images. *Black feminist thought: Knowledge, consciousness, and the politics of empowerment* (2nd ed., pp. 69–96). New York: Routledge.

Conlan, T. (2007, May 24). Channel 4 forced to air Big Brother apologies, *The Guardian.* Retrieved from http://www.guardian.co.uk/media/2007/may/24/bigbrother.channel4.

Dixon, T. L., & Linz, D. (2000). Overrepresentation and underrepresentation of African Americans and Latinos as lawbreakers on television news. *Journal of Communication, 50*(2), 131–154.

Gross, L. (2001). *Up from invisibility: Lesbians, gay men, and the media in America.* New York: Columbia University Press.

Hall, S. (1997). The work of representation. In S. Hall (Ed.), *Representation: Cultural representations and signifying practices* (pp. 13–64). London: Sage.

Hall, S. (2003). The whites of their eyes: Racist ideologies and the media. In G. Dines, & J. M. Humez (Eds.), *Gender, race, and class in media: A text-reader* (pp. 89–93). Thousand Oaks, CA: Sage.

Hooks, B. (1992). *Black looks: Race and representation.* Boston, MA: South End Press.

Jhally, S. (Director), & Hall, S. (Lecturer). (1997). Stuart Hall: Representation and the media [video]: Media Education Foundation.

Martins, N., & Harrison, K. (2011). Racial and gender differences in the relationship between children's television use and self-esteem: A longitudinal panel study. *Communication Research.* March 16, 2011.

Morgan, M., Shanahan, J., & Signorielli, N. (2009). Growing up with television: Cultivation processes. In J. Bryant, & M. B. Oliver (Eds.), *Media effects: Advances in theory and research* (3rd ed., pp. 34–49). New York: Routledge.

Noam, E. M. (2009). *Media ownership and concentration in America.* Oxford: Oxford University Press.

Ono, K. A. (2011). Critical: A finer edge. *Communication and Critical Cultural Studies, 8*(1), 93–96.

Ono, K. A. (2010). Postracism: A theory of the 'post'-as political strategy. *Journal of Communication Inquiry, 34*(3), 227–233.

Ono, K. A. (2009a). Critical/Cultural approaches to communication. In W. F. Eadie (Ed.), *21st century communication: A reference handbook* (pp. 74–81). Thousand Oaks, CA: Sage.

Ono, K. A. (2009b). Power Rangers: An ideological critique of neocolonialism. In *Contemporary media culture and the remnants of a colonial past* (pp. 71–87). New York: Peter Lang.

Ono, K. A., & Pham, V. (2009). *Asian Americans and the media.* Cambridge, UK: Polity Press.

Revoir, P. (2007, January 17). 10,000 complain over the 'racists' of Big Brother, *Daily Mail.*

Singh, A. (2007, January 15). Big bro viewers complain of racism towards Shilpa, *The Evening Standard.*

Squires, C. (2007). *Dispatches from the color line: The press and multiracial America.* Albany, NY: SUNY Press.

Tang, M. (2007). Psychological effects on being perceived as a 'model minority' for Asian Americans. *New waves: Educational research and development, 11*(3), 11–16.

Ting-Toomey, S. (2005). Identity negotiation theory: Crossing cultural boundaries. In W. B. Gudykunst (Ed.), *Theorizing about intercultural communication* (pp. 211–233). Thousand Oaks, CA.: Sage.

CPSIA information can be obtained at www.ICGtesting.com
Printed in the USA
LVOW01s1624310315

432342LV00001B/2/P